OUT OF THE
KILLING FIELDS
INTO THE LIGHT

INSPIRATIONAL INTERVIEWS WITH
MORMON CONVERTS
FROM **CAMBODIA**

OUT OF THE
KILLING FIELDS
INTO THE LIGHT

INSPIRATIONAL INTERVIEWS WITH
MORMON CONVERTS
FROM CAMBODIA

PENNE D. CONRAD

CFI
SPRINGVILLE, UTAH

This is not an official publication of The Church of Jesus Christ of Latter-day Saints. The opinions and views expressed herein belong solely to the author and do not necessarily represent the opinions or views of Cedar Fort, Inc. Permission for the use of sources, graphics, and photos is also solely the responsibility of the author.

The views expressed within this work are the sole responsibility of the author and do not necessarily represent the position of Cedar Fort, Inc., or any other entity.

ISBN 13: 978-1-59955-525-6

Published by CFI, an imprint of Cedar Fort, Inc., 2373 W. 700 S., Springville, UT 84663
Distributed by Cedar Fort, Inc., www.cedarfort.com

LIBRARY OF CONGRESS CATALOGING-IN-PUBLICATION DATA

Conrad, Penne D., 1942-2010, author.
  Out of the killing fields, into the light : interviews with Mormon
converts from Cambodia / Penne D. Conrad.
     pages cm
  Summary: When the Khmer Rouge communists took over Cambodia in 1975, they
began a reign of terror and torture that took over a million lives. A few
were fortunate enough to find sponsors in the United States and were allowed
to immigrate there and start a new life. This book contains the collected
stories of twelve of those refugees who found their way to the Church of Jesus
Christ of Latter-day Saints.
  ISBN 978-1-59955-525-6
  1. Mormon converts--Cambodia. 2. Cambodia--History--1975-1979. 3.
Christian converts from Buddhism. 4. Parti communiste du Kampuchea. I.
Title.

  BX8693.C655 2011
  289.3092'2596--dc22
  [B]

                              2010051424

Cover design by Angela D. Olsen
Cover design © 2011 by Lyle Mortimer
Edited and typeset by Kelley Konzak

Printed in the United States of America

10 9 8 7 6 5 4 3 2 1

Printed on acid-free paper

This book is dedicated to the Conrad grandchildren:
Christian, Lydia, Jacob, Sam, Sierra, Kianna, Faith,
Keely, Koby, Reese, Tessa, Megan, Sage, and Lacy.

Thanks to Cindy Harding and Walt Stone for their thoughtful assistance with the manuscript. Thanks also to Kelley Konzak at Cedar Fort. The illustrations were lovingly done by Irena Harding.

"I do not believe that sheer suffering teaches. If suffering alone taught, all the world would be wise, since everyone suffers. To suffering must be added mourning, understanding, patience, love, openness and the willingness to remain vulnerable."

—Anne Morrow Lindbergh

INTRODUCTION

There are some experiences in mortality that we prefer to forget. And sometimes when life is ripped apart, forgetfulness can even be a great blessing. But the prophet Spencer W. Kimball once said that the most important word in the English language is *remember*. He wasn't talking about simple recall; his usage was more sacramental. If to dismember is to pull apart, perhaps to re-member is to put back together in order to re-create a prior wholeness. Such remembrance can be a part of redemption.

On April 17, 1975, under the direction of their leader, Pol Pot, the Khmer Rouge communists captured the Cambodian capital city of Phnom Penh and began their four-year reign of terror that dismembered a country. They evacuated the cities and dragged off everyone to work in the rice fields in an attempt to create a purely agrarian society. The communists outlawed religion and even all unapproved family relations. Fearing discontent or rebellion against the government, they targeted intellectuals, hauled them off to the rice fields (nicknamed the Killing Fields), and executed them. They singled out anyone who could read or write or even who wore glasses. Historians estimate that during those four years of communist rule, nearly two million Cambodians died by torture, murder, and starvation, amounting to one fourth of the population.

The Khmer Rouge were defeated by North Vietnamese communists in 1979 and subsequently went underground. They continued to fight as a resistance movement well into the 1990s. North Vietnam set up a puppet government called the People's Republic of Kampuchea. But under pressure from the United Nations, the Vietnamese eventually relinquished control of the country. Cambodia has been run by a peaceful, democratically elected government since 1993.

During the atrocities from 1975 to 1979, many Cambodians tried to flee into Thailand to escape the wrath and hardships imposed by the Khmer Rouge. There they were confined to refugee camps and treated only slightly better than in the communist-run camps back home. Some who were fortunate enough to find sponsors in the United States were allowed to emigrate and start a new life. Long Beach, the most ethnically diverse city in America, was one of the primary gathering points for these refugees. A precious few culminated their journey to freedom by discovering the gospel of Jesus Christ and joining the LDS Church. The Park Branch, which later became the Park Ward, was their meeting place. That is where my parents met these Cambodian Saints while serving for fourteen years as local missionaries among their congregation.

On January 7, 2010, my mother, Penne Conrad, passed away peacefully in the presence of her family. Her life's dream was to have the opportunity to tell the stories of the Cambodian Saints she had come to love so dearly. Before she died, my mother read a draft of the transcriptions I made of her interviews. She gave her approval, and I think she was satisfied that her dream was coming true.

No one will ever know in this life the extent of the suffering of these good people. Only Christ through his Atonement can comprehend and rectify the wrongs committed against them, for truly he did "take upon him the pains and the sicknesses of his people" (Alma 7:11). The suffering and heartache of these Cambodian converts retold here has been swallowed up in the redeeming love of the Savior. Through the Atonement, they are becoming "at one" again. But sometimes it is still good to remember—to remember the trials from which the Lord has delivered us in a way that increases our appreciation of his tender mercies. This is one attempt to remember those stories.

Chad Conrad, February 1, 2011

NIKE CHAB

My name is Chheang Chab Plong, but I go by Nike. My mother is Hak Hean, and my father is Chab Plong. I am the fourth of seven children. I was basically left an orphan by the communist takeover of my country, Cambodia.

When I was four or five years old, just before the Khmer Rouge takeover, my father built a house under a huge Tamarind tree. He used bamboo as the foundation. The roof was made of a thatched rice straw. The floor was made of bamboo. The hut was four to five feet above the ground, being built on stilts to protect it when the floods came. We lived a day's travel away from the city of Battambang.

Nike's mother's house in Cambodia

Before the war, life was magical for us as children. My siblings and I went to a public school. I got to attend long enough to learn the alphabet. We were poor but happy. We invented our own instruments. We made drums. We made something out of coconuts and strings from palm leaves that made a vibrating sound like a guitar. We even had something that looked like a piano called a *khim*. It was made from bamboo and wood from a large tree and some wire.

We had to entertain ourselves as children. No one had any money to buy toys. We played a lot in the river. At least three times, I nearly drowned but was saved at the last moment. The Lord was looking out for me even as a young child. Our favorite game was called *choong*. We wrapped something up in a towel to make a small bundle about four inches in diameter. Then we played a game somewhat like American football with ten to fifteen people per side. Whichever side dropped the *choong* had to sing and dance or get their faces painted with powder and water. Our one holiday for the year was a New Year celebration. We would have a parade that would go from town to town, adding people at each stop, and then end up in one spot with a grand feast. We played games like *choong*. Except for weddings, New Year's was our one time to party. It was a very big deal!

And then the communists of the Khmer Rouge came to power. They put an end to the parties, the games, and the schooling. They put an end to our entire childhood.

Every day we were sent into the fields to work. They had us farming rice. A rice field was forty feet by sixty feet of mud. Each individual plant had to be planted, cut, and harvested one by one. Rice was our one crop. It was also our only official meal that the Khmer Rouge provided for us once a day. It was against the rules to eat anything else, but we were driven by hunger. We found whatever vegetables or fruit we could find that looked edible and mixed it in with our rice. We also hunted and fished for meat. Sometimes, if we were lucky, we would catch lizards, rats, or snakes to eat as well. They tasted like chicken. When other food was scarce, we ate cat or dog meat. We did what we had to in order to survive. My favorite food to eat was the crispy, burnt rice at the bottom of the pot. We ate it like a special snack or treat. That was all we had, so we made the best of it. We had to hide our extra food from the communists. If they caught us with unauthorized food, they would punish us physically and verbally in front of the entire village.

When the Khmer Rouge took over, they confiscated everything we had—our animals, our land, our possessions—even our fruit trees. They said from then on they would be taking care of us, so we didn't need any personal possessions. At five or six in the evening, they would ring a bell and call the whole camp together for our meal. Their cooks didn't know or didn't care how the rice tasted. They would cook it with the chaff or husk still on it. It tasted awful. It would stick to our throats and choke us. Sometimes we would volunteer to help cook just so it was edible.

The communists took away our men to serve in their army. They took my dad first. I was only five or six, so I was too young. But they took my older brother, Ploy, and he was only a few years older than me. My dad and Ploy would sneak out and return to try to help us, but the guards would catch them and take them back. I was sent every morning at dawn to work in the rice fields with my little brother, Chhay. My mom was also sent out to work in the fields but at a different location. No one was allowed to stay behind to watch my little sisters Chhuth, Poy, and Panron. All of us missed our father desperately.

Panron missed our father so much that she became very ill. She couldn't eat or drink. She lost all her weight and became nothing but skin and bones. One winter morning while my mother was holding her by the fire to try to warm her up, her tooth fell out. My mother just quietly pulled the tooth out of the ashes and told us not to cry. A few days later, I came back from the river, and they had wrapped my dead sister up in a bundle to bury her. Panron was such a beautiful and loving sister, and she had such a sweet voice. We were all devastated to lose her.

Often I would get sores and infections over my body. My mom would send me into the river up to my neck to let the shrimp and little fish clean all my wounds. They would eat all the infected skin and leave me clean again. It didn't hurt—just tickled.

I remember the first time I saw a car. It scared me. I thought it was some sort of monster. I was so distracted, I didn't watch where I was walking and got tangled in some rusted barbed wire. I was hooked in a bad way. My brother, Chhay, had to help free me. My wounds were deep and became infected. We didn't have access to any medicine or treatment of any kind. My mom covered me in white basil and saliva. The wounds finally healed up but left big scars on my back.

Chhay and I had to improvise for any kind of fun activity we could find. One time we were playing a sort of homemade hockey. I hit our makeshift puck so hard right at my brother, and it hit him between the eyes. He was bigger than me and was going to let me have it. I ran as fast and as far away as I could. I disappeared into the rice fields until after sunset. I missed the mealtime, and my mother knew I'd be terribly hungry without my one meal. She tried to sneak me a bowl of rice, but our neighbor saw what she was doing and turned her into the guards. They took her into the public square and berated her. They cursed her and threatened her. My brother and I felt horrible for what happened, but my mother never said a word to us. This wasn't our fault. We were prisoners of the Khmer Rouge and treated like animals. We learned to act dumb and follow orders. They took away all education and tried to turn us into thoughtless workers for their cause.

But we learned to survive. My brother and I got pretty good at fishing and hunting birds to eat with our slingshots. One time my brother caught one hundred birds in one day. He sat on the top of a ripened fruit tree and shot the birds coming to feast on the fruit. We decided to share some with our neighbors. We gave them ten birds to eat. They were lazy and wouldn't do any hunting themselves. They decided we hadn't shared enough with them and grew jealous. So they told the authorities. The guards came and confiscated all our food. They said they had to share it with everybody. Of course, we never saw a single bird or fish from what they took. When they slaughtered a cow, we would get a piece of meat the size of your thumb. They had us grow yams and bananas, but they would never let us eat them. You'd be beaten if you tried. Only the Khmer Rouge authorities ever got to eat food like that. One time I saw a guard eating a banana. I waited around until he threw off the peel. I then devoured his banana peel like a forbidden treat.

Finally, the fighting between the Khmer Rouge and the Vietnamese caught up to where our little concentration camp was. The bombs started going off everywhere. You could hear the machine guns. They sounded like popcorn popping. My father escaped from the Khmer Rouge army and found us again. We found a little canoe with holes in it, climbed in, and started paddling downstream away from the fighting. We filled the holes with mud and bailed out the water as we went. We kept having to replug the holes, since mud doesn't do such a good job resisting water.

We arrived at Chnom City, where my brothers and sisters, Chu, Jam, Jung, and Chud were living. We rested there for a couple of days until the fighting caught up again with us there. My mother and Ploy got into the canoe with some of our meager belongings, but the rest of us gave up on the sinking canoe and just continued walking the bank of the river. We were headed for Vietnam. But at one point, my mother and one of my brothers decided they would try to find some clothing we had dropped a little ways back. We were deep in the jungle. They never found us again. We made our way back to the village and waited for them in the rubble for two weeks hoping they'd show up, but they never did. So we took off again with only Father to lead us. This time we headed for Thailand. I wouldn't see the rest of my family again for many years.

The journey to Thailand was hard and sad. There were lines and lines of people headed in the same direction through the jungle. The further we got, the thinner and thinner the lines became. People just died off on the trail. We had nothing to eat except what we could find along the way. We would peel off the bark of trees and lick the sap. I guess it had fructose in it and gave us some energy.

My sister got very sick along the way. She started throwing up all the time. Eventually she started throwing up blood. She couldn't travel anymore. We had to leave her with her husband and two small children. But we couldn't stay. There was no food or shelter in the jungle. We were being eaten alive by the mosquitoes. We left them there and moved on.

We just kept plunging through the jungle hoping to find help in Thailand. We ate crickets, lizards, bugs, and crabs—anything that looked edible. We could build fires at night and cook things. We dug for yucca roots and yams. Some of the yams were good and some were poisonous, so we had to be very careful. But what choice did we have? It took us two or three months. At one time, I was so thirsty when we came to a pothole with polluted water in it. It smelled like cow urine. But I was dying of thirst, so I drank it. Miraculously, it didn't kill me, but I never felt really well on the journey after that. We moved on.

People were dying everywhere around us. Some were starving to death. Others were shot by the Khmer Rouge soldiers fleeing from the Vietnamese. Still others were blown to bits by land mines or caught in booby traps. Whenever I went off hunting for food for what was left of our family, I would stumble across dead bodies. But I just climbed over them and kept looking.

Several times I was left by myself in the jungle. I was five or six years old and had no idea what to do. But impressions would come to me in the moment that would get me back to the group. Often I'd feel guided to look for my family's tracks in the mud and follow them back to where they were. Looking back now, it is clear to me that I was being guided by divine providence. It's the only explanation that makes sense to me why I didn't die in the jungle while so many others around me did.

By the time we got to the Thai border, there were just my father, myself, my sisters, Chhuth and Pov, and my brother, Chhay. My father left us and went into Thailand to see what he could find. He returned and said that he found some Thai families that would take us in to live with them, but we would have to split up. My brother and I decided to try to make that work, but my sister really didn't want to leave our dad. He left her with a family anyway, and they gave him a fifty-pound bag of rice. But she cried and cried nonstop for two days. So they finally let her go. She ran after my brother and father but never caught up with them. I was afraid she had been eaten by coyotes or tigers. I didn't know what happened to her until I tracked her down in 2000. She was still living in Thailand.

My father left me with another family. They gave him a fifty-pound bag of rice too. I stayed and worked for the family for about two years. I picked cotton for them and worked on their farm. This Thai farmer had a wife and a daughter. What we didn't know is that he had another wife and two kids in another town. One day, he just got up and abandoned us for his other family. After a long time, he wrote us a letter telling us where he was and that we could come and join him if we could pay for the bus fares. We saved up for six months and then bought bus tickets to his town.

It was quite the memorable ride that I would never want to repeat. I had no food, no water, and I couldn't get off the bus to go to the bathroom. I just sat there on the bus for three or four days. Every time the bus stopped, venders would get on selling food. I saw the wife buy a little food for herself and her child, but she never gave me any. I survived somehow by scavenging around, and we finally arrived at their father's village, Surin. He sent us to live with his relatives. I farmed for them, taking care of their livestock, buffaloes, and cows. I lived with this family for about two years. I worked so hard that they made money off me by having me work for their neighbors.

One day the original guy that took me in asked if I wanted to go back to live with his first wife and daughter again. I gladly jumped at the chance. He took me by bus, and we made a three-day journey. I remembered that they didn't live that far, so I became suspicious. He took me to Bangkok instead. There he sold me as slave labor to a florescent light company. Six months later, he returned with his second wife and one of her children. He sold them to the company as well. There were many other children working there, apparently in the same situation as us.

The business owners were quite cruel. We only got three or four hours of sleep a night. They had us working the rest of the time. I was about eight or nine years old. We worked there for almost six months. We used our teeth as tools because they didn't provide any tools. I was pulling wires with my teeth all the time, and finally my teeth fell out. Eventually the factory owners called the man to come back for us and give them a refund for the money they paid. I guess I couldn't do the work very well anymore with my two front teeth missing.

The man took me back to work for his relatives again. The relatives didn't like the man and wanted me to stay permanently with them. They liked me and treated me well. But the man informed them that he was taking me back to Bangkok to sell me again. I pleaded with his relatives for help. They said I could run away. I did and found my way to some of his other relatives. But eventually he found me and took me back to sell me into slavery again.

His relatives finally had enough of this selfish man. They decided to report him to the Thai authorities. All Cambodian refugees were supposed to be in the refugee camps. One morning, one of his relatives took me to the authorities and dropped me off. She left me there and walked away. I was crying and didn't want to leave her; she had been so nice to me. Tears were streaming down her cheeks, and she kept turning back to look at me, but she just kept walking away, knowing I'd be better off there than in the hands of that man.

The authorities there put me on a bus, and I rode for an entire day to a Cambodian refugee camp in Surin. The camp was encircled with barbed wire and seemed more like a prison than anything else. When I arrived, the camp authorities announced over the speakers that an orphan had arrived and if anyone would take me in they would get an extra five scoops of rice. One grandmother in her sixties said she'd take me in. She had a family of her own but decided she wanted a grandchild. They ran a bakery business there in camp and really just wanted another worker. I worked for them for three or four months. Then they decided they didn't want me anymore because I didn't speak Thai. Another lady took me in to help her with her little business. I cooked rice, served customers, and washed the dishes. But she also made me massage her and pluck her gray hairs. I was like her personal slave. She wouldn't let me go out and play with the other children or go to school. I watched the other kids doing those things and yearned to be a part of them.

I found a friend while working at that little restaurant. His name was Phoeut, and he was an orphan like me. He took me to live with his relatives. He later found his family and left me there with his relative, Chhoeun Long. While living with Mr. Long, I went to work for a Chinese family selling porridge. I started saving up money whenever I could. I worked so hard that I got sick and injured my rib cage. While I was in the hospital, the family found the money I had been saving under my cot and spent it on food for themselves.

After many, many months of living in that refugee camp, we finally got the chance to go to the United States. Immigration officials came into the camp and took some of us to live in the States. I didn't want to go. I wanted to return to Cambodia, but we were told it was too dangerous. We were sent to two more refugee camps during the next year.

These camps were even worse than the first. Food was more scarce. I took to selling bread and gasoline each morning to earn some money to buy food. One time a Thai soldier saw me selling my wares and started whipping me violently. We weren't supposed to sell anything to make money. I saw another refugee—a little grandmother—get caught by a guard while she was trying to sell some food. She had a pot of boiling oil with her, and the guard took the pot and dumped it on her head. She died instantly where she stood, boiled in her own oil.

I was still living and moving around with Mr. Long and his family. We were sent to a refugee camp in the Philippines. We only stayed for a month or two. Some who could not pass the health examinations got stuck there permanently. Fortunately, I passed the tests and was sent to the United States with Mr. Long's family.

We arrived in Corpus Christi, Texas, and were taken to an abandoned building surrounded by wire fences. For six months, we waited there for someone to sponsor us. While we were there, I had other refugee children to play with. One day, I was walking around and playing in the abandoned buildings with the other children. I found some detached wires lying on the ground and was fascinated by them. I was intrigued with how they were made and how they functioned. When I had satisfied my curiosity, I threw the wires back on the floor. When I got back to where Mr. Long was, he was waiting for me. He took his belt off and began hitting me with it. The belt cut up my back pretty badly. I was bleeding all over. I didn't have a clue why I was being punished. Only later did I discover someone had told him I had almost started a fire playing with wires. I never even questioned what happened for fear of being punished again. But another time an old lady saw me spitting on the floor. She complained quite loudly to Mr. Long, and I was beaten again.

Finally some friends of Mr. Long landed a sponsor in Akron, Ohio. We all just went with them by bus. We stayed in Ohio for about a year, where I attended elementary school. In 1984, Mr. Long found out his best friend from the refugee camp in Surin was then living in Long Beach. So we bought bus fares to Long Beach. I got car sick and vomited the entire trip.

Once in Long Beach, I was enrolled in Franklin Junior High School and finally began learning the alphabet. I had to change schools because I was getting beaten up every day. I ended up at Hoover Junior High, where I was enrolled to take English as a second language. I had to work hard to try to catch up to where the other students were academically. I really never had any formal schooling before. But I knew how to work hard and graduated with an A average. I went on to Millican High School and did very well there. I got beaten up a lot, but I learned how to survive among all the gangs in Long Beach. I even made the school football team.

Inner-city Long Beach was like another Killing Field with all the gangs going at each other. The Crips and the Bloods were fighting all around us. There were a lot of Cambodian gangs as well. One night my best friend, Roman Lim, and I played basketball until one in the morning. Then we each headed home. On his way, he was shot in the head and killed by a gang member. I survived, but I was always getting beaten up.

One day, I was walking home from school and got to my usual turn down a long alley. Something prompted me not to go that way this time. I went on to another street. At the end of it, I saw a group of Hispanic youth coming out of the alley I would have been stuck in. They were all riding bikes and looking for trouble. When they saw me, they all headed toward me, cursing and threatening to kill me. Because of that prompting I received, I had enough extra time to respond and run away from them. I quickly climbed up the side of an apartment building and hid from them on the roof. That prompting might have saved my life.

Another time, some friends and I were playing basketball at the junior high after school. There were some kids playing on the court next to us. One of them got tired, dropped out of the game, and sat on my bag. We finished and wanted to leave, so I asked the kid to get off my bag so I could go. He said no. I asked him again, but he refused. So finally I just yanked the bag from under him, and he fell flat on his back. The next thing I knew, I had twelve people—kids, teens, and adults—on top of me, beating me to a pulp. I fought my way out of the pile and started running. There were a lot of people watching these guys beat me up, but only one person helped me. His name was Mony Kim. They smashed his jaw, but he helped me enough that I was able to get away with my life.

Mony Kim was different than any other person I had ever known. I met him in the apartment complex where I lived with Mr. Long. We were both sixteen. Mony didn't drink or smoke or take advantage of women. He was kind and polite with everybody, no matter what their ethnic background was. He had such a good spirit about him. When he asked people how they were doing, he would ask them questions until he was sure they were really doing well. I wondered why he was so different than other people. He was the most caring, loving person I have ever known. He told me he was a Mormon and introduced me to the Mormon missionaries. He started taking me to seminary, Mutual, and youth activities with him, and I loved what we were doing and what I was learning.

Before Mony started taking me to the LDS Church, I had visited and studied about lots of different churches. Running around the jungles of Cambodia and watching people get blown to bits by land mines or shot by guards, I often wondered if there was any life after death. As a teenager in America I decided I had to find out. I felt like I met a lot of sincere people, but none of the churches I had attended moved me. Only the Mormon missionaries seemed to have the answers I was looking for. They assured me that I would live again after I died, and I believed them. I started reading the Book of Mormon and praying. I was baptized in 1986 at age sixteen. When I was confirmed and received the gift of the Holy Ghost, I felt the Spirit strongly that what I was doing was right and that I was really being born again into a new life. The complex puzzle of my life was finally put together, and I could see the bigger picture. But it wasn't until I started serving as a ward missionary and later as the ward mission leader that I really saw my testimony start to grow. I guess the best way learn the truth of the Church is by serving in it.

At first Mr. Long didn't care about my involvement in the Church. As long as I did well in school and stayed out of trouble, he had no interest in what I did with the rest of my time. But after going to Long Beach Community College for a year, I decided to go on a mission. All of a sudden, Mr. Long decided that the Church was taking too much of my time. He told me that if I served a mission, I wouldn't have a place to live when I got back. I didn't care. I was called to the Dallas Texas Mission, where I served from 1990–1992. I served for six months there among the Cambodians speaking Cambodian. But then I was transferred over to work with the Laotian people. I had to learn their language. We had a lot of success bringing people to the gospel.

One time we had gathered a large, extended family of Laotians who had shown some interest in hearing our message. As we were sharing the Joseph Smith story, we started quoting his words about seeing the Father and the Son. One of the women who was lying on the floor felt the Spirit so strongly that she jumped up on her feet, almost as if she was shot into the air. Her eyes got really big, and she started looking all around her, trying to identify what was happening. We explained to her that it was the Holy Ghost testifying that our message about the First Vision was true. She became a strong witness of our message and was baptized along with about twenty of her extended family and friends. As a missionary, I saw many, many lives change for the better.

I came home to Long Beach in 1992. I finished my associate's degree in administrative justice at the city college. For years I had felt as though I needed to marry a Thai girl. Then one day I went to a young adult fireside, and after it was over, a young Thai lady I had never met didn't have a ride. I drove Montira home. It was almost as if the Lord set us up on our first date! A few months later, in 1995, I married Montira Ritcharoeun in the Los Angeles Temple, and we have been active in the Church ever since. We are raising three children in the Church, Wanchai, Melody, and Marvin. We try to help them appreciate being American as well as value their Cambodian and Thai heritages. In 1998, I was hired by the LA County Sheriff's office. We don't have much money, but we make ends meet. We are rich in spirit, and the Lord always helps us find food for our table.

In 2002, I took my wife, Montira, to Thailand to visit her family. While I was there, I went to the Cambodian embassy to look for my family. I spent all day there without any success. Finally a man there introduced me to a young woman named Da. She lived in Aran on the border between Thailand and Cambodia. I told her the name of the town where I last saw my father and brother and sister. She said she knew exactly where that was. She had a cousin who lived there. She contacted her cousin, who actually knew my family. It was a miracle!

For twenty years I had wondered what had happened to my family. I had prayed every single day for help in finding them again. They came over to the embassy and met with me. My dad and my younger sister came, and we talked. They had all ended up in different Thai refugee camps and eventually settled around the border. My dad seemed terrified of what I might do or say because he sort of sold me for twenty-five pounds of rice, but I was just delighted to see them. I also got to meet a half brother and sister.

Then my mother came to see me. Somehow she had survived the jungle with my older sister. She eventually remarried. The first thing she did when she saw me was to lift up my shirt to check the scars on my back. Then she could be sure it was me. The first thing I said to my mother was, "How old am I?" All she could remember was that I was about thirty years old. She couldn't even remember the month or day I was born. She just knew I was about two years younger than my brother. We only had a few hours to talk, but it felt so good to see them all again and know how they were doing. I gave them a little money and said good-bye. I know the Lord was the one who made this reunion possible. How grateful I am that out of my entire family, I was the one who had the chance to come to the United States and find the gospel.

I so wanted to return to visit them again, but I received word that my father and brother both passed away. I did some genealogical

Nike (second from left in front) on his trip to Cambodia, meeting sisters, nieces, and nephews for the first time

research on them and then did their temple work. My older brother was killed by the Khmer Rouge. They didn't like him because he was such a good hunter. One day they put a land mine in the path he always took hunting and blew him up. I went to the temple and did his work as well. I did get to visit my mother again before she died, and I'm grateful for that blessing. I keep in touch now the best I can with all my siblings back in Cambodia.

At times it has been hard to forgive those who treated me so poorly throughout my life. But it has been the Atonement of Christ that has helped me let go of the pain and the resentment and replaced them with love and forgiveness. They did a lot worse to Christ than anyone ever did to me, and he was able to forgive. So somehow I have to learn to forgive as well. I am so grateful that the Lord rescued me from my chaotic upbringing and provided a path for me to enjoy his glorious gospel.

People trust way too much in money to find happiness and security in this life. Many learn too late that money brings more sorrow and problems than it solves. Gratitude for our blessings is really the way to find happiness in life. We are so blessed to have the gospel. I know— I'm the only one in my family who has it. Now we just have to show our gratitude by truly living the principles we understand. We have to learn to reach out in love and acceptance to those who don't understand God's plan and let them feel His love through us. They really are our brothers and sisters, so it's time we start treating them like family. When we do, we'll find the happiness and security we seek.

Nike with his daughter, Melody

NHEAN KIM

When I was a little girl, we had a wonderful, simple life together as a family. My parents were Leang and Ngua, and I had two brothers, Khun and Hal. But then Father passed away when I was seven, and things became very, very hard. My mother, Ngua, didn't seem to know how to survive without Father. She simply fell apart. My little brothers stayed with her, but I was taken to live with my Uncle That. My uncle was away working most of the time, and my aunt didn't treat me very well. She just fed me a little rice every day—barely enough to keep me alive. But she worked me hard like a servant and was very mean to me. Eventually I ran away from my aunt and uncle. I was sent to live with another aunt and uncle. Things were a lot better with them. I worked from dawn to dusk selling cookies and groceries, but they were nice to me and treated me tenderly. When I was twelve, my uncle stopped working, so they couldn't afford to feed me anymore. They sent me back to live with my mom and brothers.

I didn't spend much time at home. I would eat meals with the neighbors and hang out with them most of the time. I would babysit their kids during the day, and then in the evening, they took me to see plays or whatever they were doing. They treated me like one of the family. No one had very much. Everybody was poor. Just some were poorer than others. I sold fish and vegetables and fruit—anything to make money and help out.

My mom never was able to raise me. When my Uncle That remarried, I was sent back to live with them. It still wasn't very pleasant for me there, but I got along the best I could.

When I was fourteen, my family decided that I should get married. The man was eighteen, and I didn't love him. It was a hard life. I had no support from my mother or from his family. In fact, his family was quite cruel to me. My husband went to school, and I stayed home with a baby girl at age fifteen. I had two more boys and then another girl named Lith. When my oldest was nine, my mother-in-law decided she wanted to raise her for a while. So without my consent, she was taken, and she lived with her grandma for about a year. Then something happened, and my daughter died. They never told me what happened. You can imagine how horrible it all was for me. It was like my soul was torn from me. I didn't think life could get any worse.

Then the Khmer Rouge came in and took over. Everything changed. They took our house, our car, and our possessions. All they left us with was a blanket and a few clothing items. They said they were going to relocate us and took us on a journey through the jungle. But finally they just dropped us off and left us in the jungle with the lions and tigers. We wandered for two or three months, hiding from the animals and scraping up anything we could find to eat. It was a miracle we came through alive.

Finally we were captured and taken to one of the Khmer Rouge camps. We lived there for four years in total poverty and virtual slavery. There were no gates around the camp we were in, but there were guards everywhere who would shoot you if you tried to leave. My husband was a doctor but had to pretend he was an ignorant farmer. If he would have been wearing glasses, they would have killed him. That was one way they identified people who were smart and had an education. They separated the men from the women in our camp, and everyone spent all day, every day working in the rice fields. In our camp, they allowed us to eat two small bowls of rice a day—in the morning and at night. That was more than most people had to live on. But it was not enough. We grew so skinny and malnourished that we looked like all those pictures of Jewish Holocaust victims you see. I found a hidden spot to grow a few vegetables. They were covered with bugs that would bite anyone else who tried to steal them. But for some reason they never bit me. I guess even in the midst of this hellhole, the Lord was watching over me. We survived there for two to three years.

The worst part of living in that camp was watching so many people being executed. I saw my mother-in-law executed for having an affair with the father of one of the Khmer Rouge. There were never any trials, and no evidence was required. She had her ankles tied to oxen that were driven in opposite directions and her body was torn in half. They wanted to make an example of her. They executed her entire family as well. My father escaped into the jungle, and I never saw him again.

Finally the Vietnamese took over the country from the Khmer Rouge. We were given a little more freedom under the Vietnamese communists than we had under the Cambodian ones. We made a little money making and selling gemstones.

But several months later, things started growing worse for us. The guards kept making life more and more difficult. We finally decided to escape into Thailand. When we got there, the Thai soldiers drove us back to Cambodia. They just dumped us all off there in an unknown jungle to die. We walked through rivers, forests, and even minefields back to our home. It took us over a month of wandering in the jungle, but we survived. We were blessed. Many others died along the way.

Many months later, we were ready to try to escape to Thailand again. My older sons went with my husband in a separate group. It was the only way we could arrange our escape. I came later, carrying my baby, Lith, in my arms. At one point, a gang of young men with guns came to attack and rob our little group. Some of them raised their guns at my head. All of a sudden, two men dressed in white appeared behind me. They told the boys to leave. They all fled as fast as they could. Thanks to those two men in white, we all made it over the border into Thailand. The Lord was watching out for us all along the way. Still, there was no rest. We were caught by Vietnamese soldiers, put in a truck, and carted back to the Cambodian wilderness.

We stayed for a while where they dropped us off, trying to figure out what to do. Water was a problem. It took a day to fetch one gallon of water. I felt sorry for so many other families that didn't have any water. I gave a bowl of water to the family next to us. My husband was angry, but I told him I could find some more.

I took off up a hill to look for more water. Several people followed after me. At the top of the hill, I saw a turtle. It was so thin and scrawny from not getting any food or water itself that I felt bad for it. I didn't have the heart to catch and eat it. I shoved it into the bushes because I knew anyone else who saw it would catch it for food. Next I saw a little crab crawl out of the bushes, and I felt the same way. But the crab had been sitting by a tiny ditch of water only a few inches long. I called to all the people following me and told them to bring their bowls. I filled every bowl and pot with water. Later, after I had joined the Church and read the story of Christ feeding the multitudes with fishes and loaves, I thought about giving water to all those people from that two-inch little ditch. I've seen many miracles in my life.

We had no idea where to go. I prayed all night long for help. The only thing I knew to pray to was Buddha, but I was totally sincere. Finally, I fell asleep and had a dream. In the dream, an old lady carrying a blue lamp came and said, "Follow me." In my dream, I walked through the minefields following the old lady. We walked for miles and miles.

The next morning we set off and followed the exact path I had seen in my dream. We saw an old church building I had seen in my dream. We walked past many people blown up by land mines and just lying along the roads. There were times that angels led us away from the mines and saved our lives. It took us over a month to get back to our home in Cambodia. We had so little to eat. I was depressed and desperate for my baby. But the Lord helped us through. We were anxious to be rid of the cruel communist rule. Soon we took off for the Thai border again.

Twice we were held up by the Khmer Rouge. They would have killed me if they found the gold I was carrying under my clothes. Both times I held up Lith and said, "Do you want to search us? Go ahead, start with me!" And then I started to take my clothes off. As soon as I started this big show, they pushed by me and searched everyone else. Fortunately, both times nobody was killed. We finally reached the Thai border a second time.

The challenge was to get across the border. We had to run across an open area without getting shot by the Thai border patrols. If you survived the crossing, you could get safely into Thailand. But my baby, Lith, was bigger and heavier now. Everyone started running and left me and my baby to fend for ourselves. A Chinese man saw my problem when I fell with Lith. He picked us up and helped us across the border. I gave the man some gold so he could bribe the guards. The way the refugee camps were run, you couldn't just walk in. We had to sneak into camp. For a while, we had to hide under refugees' beds to escape the guards. Eventually we were able to find the right guards to bribe with my gold and achieved official refugee status.

Life in the refugee camp was better than under the Khmer Rouge, but we still had guards who took advantage of us. From the Thai camp, we went to the Philippines. There we lived in a village where there were no guards. There was a much more optimistic feeling there since we were all waiting for sponsors to the United States. My husband had an uncle in New York and had made his way there. Finally he was able to send for us, and we arrived at Shrub Oaks, New York.

We were sponsored by a Presbyterian church there in Shrub Oaks. Just as things started looking up for our displaced family, my husband cheated on me and took the boys to live in California. So Lith and I lived in Shrub Oaks for a year by ourselves. But the people were all ritzy, upper-class Americans. They were nice to us, but we didn't feel like we fit in. We found a Cambodian community in the Bronx on Andrew Avenue, so we moved there. In the Bronx, we were surrounded by our culture and got to speak our language and eat our food, but the living conditions were unsafe. You couldn't even walk down your own street at night without being fearful for your life. It was almost like the fear of living around the Khmer Rouge again. So we had to find another place to live.

My husband had relatives in California, and I decided to take a two-week trip there with Lith. It felt good to be surrounded by family, so we decided to stay. We got an apartment in Long Beach in the Cambodian part of town and finally felt like we had found our home.

While living in Long Beach, I had another dream. I saw three missionaries walking along a field of grass near the ocean. They had on white shirts and name tags. Some time later, I saw the Mormon missionaries near the beach just as I had seen them in the dream. I ran up to them and almost knocked them over with excitement. They taught me the gospel and almost immediately, I accepted it all. I had been

Buddhist my whole life but never really found much comfort in the rituals of our religion. Somehow I always knew there was a God and had found answers to my prayers many times. So praying about the Church came naturally to me, and I soon knew I had found the truth. I was baptized in October of 1991. It was the greatest day of my life.

My daughter, Lith, was baptized as well. She eventually served a mission for the Church in New York. Ironically, or perhaps by the Lord's design, she served in the two areas we had lived in while in New York—Shrub Oaks and the Bronx. She got to teach a lot of Cambodians, including people we had known before. Babysitters, neighbors, and friends were all willing to listen to this Mormon missionary they had known as a little girl. Most of her success, though, was with Hispanics, African Americans, Filipinos, and people from the Dominican Republic. Our experiences prepared her to teach people how the Savior rescues lost souls.

Our life has been so much better since we found the gospel. We still have challenges, but now we know how to handle them better. I suffer from advanced diabetes and can't get out to do much. But now we have hope of a better life to come. We never really had that before.

Nhean with her daughter, Lith, at Temple Square

SAY LY

My name is Say Ly. I was born in Battambang, Cambodia, in the year 1940. I was the second oldest of five children. We lived in a simple bamboo hut and had to entertain ourselves with little games we made up with balls or sticks. We played games with the animals—pretending we were cowboys with the cows. My dad was a humble farmer, and we all had to work hard. We ate mostly rice and fish. I received an elementary education at the local monastery and then went into the military at age twenty-nine. When the Khmer Rouge took over, I left the military and returned to farming, trying to blend in and not be noticed by the Khmer Rouge. Anyone they discovered that had been in the military before the takeover was executed.

Saray Ean, my wife, was born in Battambang in 1954. She also grew up in a humble bamboo hut. Her father was a farmer until he was drafted by the military. Saray helped her family make a living by growing various plants in their yard and selling them for food in the market. Other plants grew wild near their home that could be picked and sold at the market.

I met Saray when she was sixteen. I was thirty-one. We met through a mutual friend. We were married in 1970. My wife had three miscarriages and then finally a child was born. But we lost it as a baby.

Once the Khmer Rouge came to power in 1975, everything changed. Our food was rationed. We were given a little bowl of rice porridge to eat twice a day, and that was about all we had. We were separated from our families and friends and sent to where they needed

us. We had to work where they told us to work, doing what they told us to do. For days we had to dig irrigation ditches all day. If you didn't finish your assigned four-foot-by-four-foot segment of the ditch by the end of the work day, you couldn't sleep until you did. Anyone who made trouble could be executed. Almost every day, they asked us if we had been in the military. You had to lie. Using spies, trick questions, and random guesses, they found people they thought might have been military and took them off for execution.

Most of our neighbors and relatives were killed. Eventually we fled to Thailand as refugees. We had a pot and two pounds of rice with us. It took us two days to get there, dodging land mines the whole way. We just prayed to God that we'd make it safely. Once we got to the border, it became even harder. The Thai guards were waiting at the gates and watching for refugees. If they caught you, they would take you to prison and perhaps even kill you. Our family all made it across, but others in our large group of refugees turned back. And we saw many others shot there at the border.

We lived in Thailand for four years. I worked with local utilities, pumping water and such. They paid us with food. Since we didn't have any children, we adopted a child there. Saray raised pigs and sold them to make money to buy milk to feed the baby.

Life in Thailand as refugees was very harsh. Rice and fish were rationed. We'd be given food once a week, but it would only last three days. So we had to find ways to stretch our rations and find other things to eat. People would steal from each other, trying to survive. The conditions brought out the worst in people sometimes.

We heard that the United States started accepting Cambodian refugees into the country, so we filled out the proper forms and prayed we'd be accepted. We were moved from one refugee camp, Caladon, to Chamboree, and we stayed there six months. Finally, we were accepted by the US government.

We were sponsored by a Baptist church in Norwalk, California, in 1983. We moved to Long Beach three months later. I took technical classes in electronics and worked in that field for several years. But I had surgery on my hands and can't do the work much anymore.

We are raising seven kids now in Long Beach—grandchildren and nephews—along with our adopted Thai son. We started attending different churches, looking for help for our children. We just didn't find anyone with a practical message. Then Mormon missionaries knocked on our door once, and we sent them away. But they came back again, and this time I decided to listen. I knew we needed help in raising all these kids, and I thought maybe the Mormons would have something that would help. They sure did! We were all baptized in 2005. Elder Burr and Elder Freebairn taught us and then Elder Romreill baptized me. Then I received the Aaronic priesthood and baptized my family. It changed our lives forever. We went to the Los Angeles Temple and were sealed as an eternal family on April 11, 2006.

Our children didn't have any direction in life until we found the Church. Now with Sunday lessons and Mutual and Scouting, we all have direction and unity as a family. Even our twenty-three-year-old adopted son, who was living away, returned to us and has gotten involved. The Church really saved our family. Now I know that Joseph Smith was a true prophet. I know the Book of Mormon is true because I've read it and prayed about it. I know the leaders of the Church are inspired and teach the messages we need to hear today. We try to go to the temple each month, and I always feel the Spirit when we go. Our grandchildren now go to seminary and can't wait to serve missions. Some people think it's hard to live the life of a Mormon. It really isn't. Our lives are much easier now with the gospel to show us how to solve our problems.

You'd think we'd miss our home country of Cambodia. It really is a beautiful land with a rich culture. But since our birth, we saw nothing there but war and violence and bloodshed. We don't really miss anything about it. Our family and relatives are here in the States now, so there really isn't any reason to go back to Cambodia. Everything that is good in our lives has happened here, so here we will stay. We thank the Lord every day that he brought us here to this free land and to his Church.

SOKCHEAT LEE STEWART

I was born in Phnom Penh, Cambodia, on April 21, 1957. My father was San Ly, and my mom was Sophonna Mak. I was born to a large family, the third of ten children. My father was in the Cambodian army, and my mother was a housewife trying to keep up with all of us children. My father was transferred a lot by the military, so we got used to moving. Sometimes we lived on military bases. We went to school in the small villages near the bases. Later on, my folks sent one of my older brothers and me to the capital city of Phnom Penh to live with my grandmother and go to school there, so we didn't have to move around. They would visit us once a month. My mother told me that my oldest brother died when he was five years old (from sickness). I was about three years old then. My other brother, one year older than me, was killed during the civil war in 1978 (he was around twenty-two years old back then).

When I was in high school, my dad went back to school for two years as part of his advancement to lieutenant colonel. Dad always emphasized to us that education was the key to our future. He said that people could take away your wealth and possessions, but no one could ever take away your knowledge and your character. He was a role model for a lot of people, including me. Later on, after he retired from the army, he went into politics and was elected to the Cambodian Congress. Our family finally found some stability and could all live together in the capital city. Ironically, that was when the civil war broke out from 1970–1975. During the war, my father had bodyguards assigned to our family to protect us. One would drive us to school, and one would protect us at home. One would drive my father to the congressional building, and one would drive my mother around.

Our home in Phnom Penh was made of brick and wood and was fairly nice by contemporary Cambodian standards. We had indoor plumbing and a gas stove—amenities that were considered luxuries. But our refrigerator was still small—only large enough to hold some water and milk. So we still went to the market once or twice a day to get enough food for such a large family.

We were a very religious family. We were Buddhists, of course. My parents were very devout. We would go to the Buddhist temple weekly and celebrate all the holidays. My dad also built a shrine on our property. I would come home from school to help my mom feed the monks lunch every day, and then I would return and finish my day at school. My parents taught us to pray, and we knew that there were higher powers that helped guide our lives.

With the onset of the civil war, there was a lot of unrest in the countryside. Many of my father's relatives came to live with us and work in the military. Father got them jobs working at military head-quarters with him. My grandparents and three uncles, with their families of four to six children each, all moved in. Father was always adding on bedrooms to the end of our house to make more room for them. We spent a lot of time just looking for enough food to feed all the people living with us. My dad didn't make enough money from the military to support so many people living in our home, so he opened his own busi-ness. He bought large electric looms and made clothes and cloth to sell.

A lot of leaders in the military became rich by taking bribes. Busi-nessmen and others would pay them for protection or to look the other way from their illegal operations. Much lower–ranking officials in the army than my dad made lots and lots of money. Many people came to our home looking to my dad for that kind of help. But he refused them all. He told them they had to suffer the consequences for their activities. My father was the most honest man I knew.

My father started working with the help of the Red Cross to pro-vide needed food and medical supplies to the villages. The Khmer Rouge were in charge but simply did a poor job of taking care of the people's needs. Many of the military leaders became rich by stealing the Red Cross supplies and selling them on the black market. But my father had integrity and felt he had a duty to help the people. Supplies were continually dropped off at our house for delivery to the villages. We had two rooms that my father turned into a warehouse to store all the supplies that were sent. Then twice a month, Father would go by helicopter and deliver it all to people living in the countryside.

During the time of the civil war from 1970–1975, the country was in a lot of chaos. There were guns everywhere. Our home was always filled with military personnel and their weapons. Bombs planted by the Khmer Rouge were always exploding in markets, theaters, schools, and homes in the capital city. Artillery rounds and rockets were lobbed into the city from the surrounding countryside. We thought it would never end. We just kept going to school, trying to live as much of a normal life as possible.

Finally, on April 17, 1975, the Khmer Rouge prevailed and took over the country. The government saw what was happening, and many of the leaders tried to leave the country. The president, Lon Nol, was a good friend of my father. Before the government fell, President Nol told my father that he could arrange an escape for our family to the United States. But my father felt a strong duty to his parents and brothers who lived with us and depended on him. Twice he refused offers by President Nol to leave unless he were permitted to take the entire family with him. This request could not be granted.

When the Khmer Rouge took over the capital, they cleared everyone out of the city. They said they just wanted to check the city for foreign spies, and then within three days we could all return. So they told us to leave everything and just take clothing and food for three days. My dad had a lot of military vehicles and nice cars, but he left them all behind. He sensed the danger that we faced because of his status in the community and knew that we would have to conceal our former social and financial situations. He said we couldn't give them any clues as to who we were. So we all crammed into one of his old, beat-up delivery trucks—Mom, Dad, Grandma, Grandpa, and nine children—and drove out of town with the rest of the population.

My dad took two large parachutes with us to use as tents. In the middle of April, it was already quite hot. The sun beat on us all and made the journey miserable. Scores of people camped under our parachutes. One was white and could protect about thirty people from the sun. The other was camouflage and could protect around fifty people.

So we had a lot of folks around us as we camped along the way on our supposed three-day journey.

But they never let us return. They just kept marching us further and further away from Phnom Penh. Dad kept instructing us to play dumb. He had been fighting the Khmer Rouge for several years. He knew their nature and what was in store for us. Anyone who was educated or had been in the military would be killed. So he told us not even to let them know we could read or write. He told me that if anything happened to him, I was to take care of the family. Dad was such an important political figure in the old regime that he knew he would be killed. Within a day or two of our forced exodus, he went to look for food for us, and he never returned.

When my dad didn't come back to our parachute, I went out looking for him. I searched and searched the huge caravan of refugees but couldn't find him. Crying, I stumbled into one of the tents of the Khmer Rouge who were driving us all like cattle. They demanded to know what I was doing there. I told them I was desperate to find my dad who didn't come back to our tent. But they acted like they didn't believe me. They accused me of being a spy and cocked their guns as if to shoot me. I ran off, searching frantically for my father until it was so dark that I couldn't see anything. Somehow, I made it back to our camouflage parachute. But I never found any trace of my father. We never saw him again or found out what happened to him. I'm sure the Khmer Rouge figured out who he was and killed him. We also never discovered what happened to the rest of our relatives. But I fulfilled my dad's charge to care for our family. Once I was established in the United States, I sponsored my mom and each of my siblings so they could immigrate here as well.

The Khmer Rouge finally admitted to us we weren't going to go back to the city. They just sort of set us on our own to find some place to live in the countryside with armed guards posted everywhere along the roads. We decided to head for my father's hometown. We hoped to find some of his relatives there who could take us in. We met a naval officer who was carrying two huge suitcases of military clothing. He said he could help us get to the village. He would trade pieces of clothing for rice for us to eat along the way. If it hadn't been for his kindness, we never would have survived. He took us to my father's village and then left to go find his family. We were a whole nation of slaves and refugees.

The Khmer Rouge had taken control of my Father's home village, turning it into a kind of concentration camp. Now they took complete control of our lives. They told us what we were to plant, when we were to work—even what we were to wear. They decided that we couldn't wear colored clothes anymore. The only color allowed was black. There was a certain fruit tree that grew around the village that could be mashed, added to a pot of water, and then used to soak your clothes in to turn them black. So we dyed everything we had. We had only the one pair of sandals on our feet. When they wore out, we just had to go on our bare feet. There was no way for us to buy a new pair. Nobody had any money, and there was no market. Walking in bare feet to and from the farms, our feet became badly calloused. All my clothes were worn out and had to be continually patched. Since all the clothing was dyed black, no one noticed my numerous patches.

They sent us all to work on farms all day, every day. They would come by as early as 2:00 a.m. to wake us up and march us to the farms. At night, they required us to attend classes to indoctrinate us in communist theory. They taught us to sing songs about the party. They taught us to hate foreigners—especially Americans. They separated us from our families and had us live with our age and gender groups. They fed us with rice porridge. After the harvest was over, they just gave us a broth without any substance at all. We were all starving. But if you were too sick to work, they would just kill you. Anyone who came from a rich family or a prominent family was punished severely. The Khmer Rouge controlled everything. They owned everything—even your life. The communists didn't care for our welfare. We were just slaves used to run their new economic system. I didn't understand how anyone could be so cruel and unfeeling toward others.

At one point, I was so sick I couldn't stand up anymore. Even though we knew it was dangerous to admit you were sick, I had to go to the health clinic. For the entire village, there was one small room turned into a clinic and run by the Khmer Rouge. There were fifty people crammed into that little room. The nurse finally came to check me and didn't even have a thermometer to check my temperature. She just felt my forehead. I was cold and clammy. No matter what the problem was, the treatment was the same for all fifty of us. They said they were giving us a vitamin shot. But it was just water out of an old Coke bottle. They had only one old rusty needle and shot us all with that. We could have gotten hepatitis or malaria or whatever, but they didn't care. All I really needed was rest and real food. They were working us sixteen hours a day, seven days a week.

Before the communists' takeover, my grandfather ran a huge machine shop in that village. He employed over three hundred workers. Now that the communists had taken over everything, things had changed. Most of the local leaders of the village had once worked for my grandfather. They knew he was a good man. He always had extra food he gave away to anyone who needed it. But now, to win the favor of the communists, they all denounced him as a greedy, rich employer. And all of his relatives were condemned simply for being "evil" rich people. Night after night, they would take us for interrogation. They would tell us we better keep our noses clean or they would make us pay. Every day numerous people would disappear—taken away and killed by the Khmer Rouge. We never knew which day would be our day.

Sometimes I just prayed that I could die, and then I wouldn't have to endure all this inhumanity. Three times the village leaders arranged a marriage for me, and all three times I ran away and hid. I didn't want to get married. I wanted out of that hell we were living in. I wanted the freedom to pursue my education and to practice my religion. Being forced to do hard labor night and day like animals, being separated from my family with barely any food to eat, being clothed with scraps of clothing providing no protection for the body, getting married was the last thing on my mind.

Anyone who tried to practice religion was taken away. Just being seen praying in public could get you killed. My mom built a secret little shrine where we could worship and kept it hidden from the Khmer Rouge. They probably would have killed her if they had found it. They had spies who would try to find you praying in private too. You couldn't even cry. They would label you as a troublemaker and "take care of it."

The Khmer Rouge would always try to identify anyone who could read and take them away. Guards of the Khmer Rouge would come up to me all the time and say, "Here, read me this letter." I would lie and say, "No, I can't read." They'd say, "With a rich father like yours, how could you not read?" I'd say with a blank stare, "He was just raising me to be an obedient housewife." I knew Cambodian, French, and English. Before the communist takeover, I had my passport to go to the United States to attend medical school. But now I had to pretend to be ignorant and dumb or they would have taken me away and executed me. It was worse than a nightmare. It was real.

The Khmer Rouge controlled the country from 1975 to 1979. Then the Vietnamese communists came in, ran the Khmer Rouge out of the countryside, and took over control from 1979 to 1993. After the Khmer Rouge were kicked out, some of us were allowed back in the capital city of Phnom Penh. The communists had taken over our house and turned it into a headquarters of some sort, so we had to find another place to live. My brother, Chhan, and sister, Peov, had both died in 1977 at the hands of the Khmer Rouge during their captivity. Approximately fifty other family members—grandparents, aunts, uncles, and cousins—never returned to the city and are presumed to be dead. Our lives were in ruin. My dad said I had to take care of the family when he was gone, so I worked hard to do that. I learned how to fish, to build bamboo huts for us to live in, to do whatever was necessary to survive.

My mother arranged a marriage for me on September 2, 1979. A year later, I had a baby, who I named Soktheas (Scotty). I couldn't bear the thought of raising a family under communist rule. We never would have a chance at any decent life. So we saved up a little money to pay for our escape. We would try to reach a United Nations refugee camp just across the border in Thailand.

In March of 1981, we took the train to Battambang. We crammed in with hundreds of refugees. We hired a man at the border to guide us through the jungle and into Thailand and the refugee camp. He rode us on a bicycle for three days through the jungle. I was pregnant at the time with my daughter, Charya, but wasn't aware of my condition. Getting into the refugee camp was not an easy thing to do. The camp was officially closed to additional refugees in 1981, even though there were hundreds and thousands still trying to get in. We tried several times to breach the barbed-wire fence but failed (sometimes at the point of a gun). Going back to hide in the jungle was just as dangerous, for we were surrounded by Khmer Rouge soldiers, robbers, land mines, and wild animals (like mountain lions)—all threatening our destruction.

One day we decided to make another attempt to enter the camp. We left early in the morning before the sun came up. We were a small, pathetic group of wanderers just trying to become refugees in a camp that didn't want us. When we got to the fence, I went first, with my baby wrapped to my chest. All of a sudden, I heard everyone behind me

take off back into the jungle. I looked up to see a Thai guard standing over me with his AK-47 gun pointed at me, ready to shoot. I turned and tried to scramble away, but I had lost my flip-flops by this time. My feet were black and swollen, and all I could do was slowly hobble. I knew I had no hope of escape.

Just then, my baby's little arm fell out of the wrap I was holding him in. The guard must have been touched by the sight of that little arm. He said, "Go, go!" and so I hurried off back into the jungle and found my group. They said when they looked back and saw me with the guard pointing his gun at me, they all just prayed for my protection. I was grateful to be alive to protect my baby, but we still had no way to get into the refugee camp.

It took us three days and three nights to travel and to finally enter the Khoa I Dang Refugee Camp. We failed to get into the camp on the first attempt (at dawn). The Thai guard who let me escape back to the jungle found us in our little hiding place. He told us that he would return at midnight for his next shift. He also told us to wait for his return and that he would let us into the camp without harm. But it did not happen the way it should have. At the gates, there were a few other guards on duty that had to be bribed to let us in. That bribe money was the best investment I've ever made.

The guards searched us, looking for any other money or valuables they could take from us before letting us in. The only thing I had of value was an emerald ring. I hid it in the seam of my baby's tattered little shirt. The guards checked all our clothing—even the baby's—but found nothing. The ring stayed miraculously hidden. Later in camp I was able to trade the ring for milk that helped keep her alive. Once again, the Lord was watching over us.

For nearly two days straight, I prayed that God would let my baby stay asleep so we could get into the camp undetected. Miraculously, she did. But as we were crossing through the gates, she awoke and started to cry. Everyone knew her cries were going to wake up other guards, and we would all be discovered. The guard helping us demanded that I shut her up. But what could I do? I told him we hadn't had anything to eat or drink for two days. He ran off and came back with a canteen of water for us. I still remember how good that water tasted. It was like manna from heaven. He also gave me something wrapped up in a banana leaf to feed my baby. That was enough to satisfy her, and she went back to sleep. We were able to finish sneaking into camp without waking anyone unfriendly to our cause. I don't know why that guard was so kind to us. Maybe he was an angel sent by God to help us survive. At least he was an angel to us. Without him, we never would have made it. Our lives were on the line.

Even though we were inside the fence of the camp, we had no legal status there. The people who ran the camp did not know we were there and were not on the "guest list" for dinner. After a few days, I met an old friend whose brother was a group leader in the camp organization. He indicated that for a "gratuity," he could make our status official. Gaining official status in the camp was a big step in attaining our ultimate goal.

Once we had official status, we received two buckets of water a day and a minimum ration of rice and dried, salty fish. Our future began to look more promising. Because I spoke English fairly well, I was hired to translate for the health workers caring for the refugees. After being on this job for two months, I was hired as the administrator of the central care center. Soon after, I gave birth to a healthy daughter, Charya. My life finally took a turn for the better.

My husband had relatives in the United States, so we could apply to emigrate with them as our sponsors. That was our intention all along. A cousin, who lived in Salt Lake City, had agreed to sponsor us as immigrants, and we began the long and tedious process filing applications and dealing with the bureaucracy of Immigration Services. After several months, the paperwork was completed and approved, and we moved out of the refugee camp in Thailand to an immigration processing camp in the Philippine Islands. At that camp, we completed medical testing and cultural orientation, which included language classes. Soktheas was now two years old and Charya was one.

We were pretty excited on the day we boarded the plane and took off for the United States. We landed in San Francisco, changed planes, and flew on to Salt Lake City, where our cousin (and sponsor) lived. Salt Lake City was a complete shock. We landed in the city in the dead of winter, and neither I nor the children were prepared for the cold weather. We didn't have any warm clothing, and, if not for the kindness of others, we may have frozen to death.

If I were to succeed in America, I knew that I would need to continue my education. The emphasis my father always put on school still rang through my mind. On the morning after we arrived, I began walking the streets of Salt Lake City in search of a school that I might attend. With a little help from others, I finally located the Salt Lake City Adult Community High School. It was a school especially designed to help foreign students get a high school diploma. It was a perfect school for me and was within walking distance of our small basement apartment that we shared with our cousin. I had graduated from high school in Phnom Penh, but the diploma didn't represent sufficient achievement to get me into college in the States. I enrolled and immediately became engrossed in its academic program. I hadn't had any education since the Khmer Rouge had run us out of the capital city of Phnom Penh. It was good to be back in school. I graduated with my high school diploma in just six months.

At the high school, I met several other foreign students, including some Cambodians who had immigrated ahead of me. Several of these students had become members of various Christian churches in the Salt Lake City area. I still adhered to the Buddhist religion but was open to looking at different religions, especially Christianity. A couple of the Cambodian students invited me to attend two different churches with them, and I accepted their invitations. The pastor at one of the churches realized that I was new to the congregation and offered to baptize me on the spot. I turned him down but kept going. I attended the churches with an open mind but was not impressed with any of them. I told a Cambodian friend at school about my experiences with the various churches, and she suggested that I attend church with her on Sunday. She said that she was a member of The Church of Jesus Christ of Latter-day Saints, also known as the Mormons. I accepted her invitation.

The trip to church with my new friend on the next Sunday would change my life. I found the members to be friendly and felt the Spirit of God in rich abundance. I was seriously seeking a new church that would satisfy my religious yearnings. As I walked into Sunday School, I heard a voice whisper in my ear, "Child, this is what you've been looking for." I turned to see who was talking to me, but no one was there. Again I heard the voice say, "My daughter, this is what you've been looking for." I had found the Gospel of Jesus Christ and knew that it was true. I went home and prayed about it and knew that I had to join the Church. I eagerly met with the missionaries, completed the prescribed lessons, and was baptized in December of 1983. The missionaries were English-speaking, and they asked if I would be willing to accompany them as they took the gospel to the Cambodians in the Salt Lake City area. I readily agreed to help and spent many evenings translating the gospel message from English to Cambodian. It was just the beginning of my missionary efforts.

The first quiz I took in my adult high school class was a disaster. I failed miserably. I had been a straight A student in Cambodia, so I was devastated. I knew I was going to need divine assistance to succeed in America. So I told the Lord I needed the Spirit to teach me. Next, I read in the Book of Mormon and sought for the Spirit to be with me. Then I read my books and did my homework. I followed this pattern for the rest of my schooling and quickly began getting straight A's again. The Lord can even help you in school if you let him.

After I graduated from high school, I continued to look toward the future. But I wasn't sure what I should do to best help my family. One night I had a dream. In the dream, I was walking in the dark. Then I saw a barn that was surrounded with light. The door opened to me, so I walked inside. There I saw bookshelves covered with books. They looked hard and intimidating. But I heard a voice that said, "If you read these books, this light will be yours." I then went a little further into the barn. I saw more bookshelves. This time there were tables around them with people studying at them. They were doctors and lawyers and other professionals. Each was reading and each was shining with the same bright light. Then I heard again the voice. It said, "If you read these books, this light will be yours. You will become one of these brightest lights." I woke up from the dream knowing I had to continue my education at all costs.

I could not envision attending college in Utah, so I made a decision to move to Southern California, where I could utilize the community college system that existed there. So I set a date for my departure, paid my rent up to that day, rented and packed a trailer, prepared my family for the move, and was ready to depart. But the weather was still working against us. On the day we were to begin our trip to Southern California, a blinding snowstorm hit Utah. The sister missionaries that I had worked with during my stay in Utah begged me not to go and to wait instead for better weather. But I had no choice; I had already moved out of our apartment and had packed everything we owned into the trailer. We had no place to stay. I had another worry about the trip, though. The little car that we owned was not in good mechanical condition, the heater and defroster were not working, and it was really not big enough to tow the trailer we had rented. I had no money for car repairs. But I had to go. I was sure that God would get us safely to our destination.

The trip to Southern California was a nightmare. We nearly froze to death. And because the defroster was not working, we could hardly see the road in front of us. Additionally, my husband was not experienced in driving in inclement weather—much less a snowstorm. During the trip, the car went into an uncontrolled skid and slid off of the road, and the trailer turned over. With some help from a highway patrolman and a tow truck driver, we got the trailer upright and the car out of the snowbank and then were able to continue on our trip. Later in the trip, the roads became so icy that the car lost traction and we had to pull off the road for our own safety. We decided to wait in the car and not try to travel until the weather improved. While we were waiting in the car shivering from the cold, a young couple stopped and asked if we were okay. We told them that the car's heater was not working and we were sort of stranded. They could see that our situation was somewhat desperate, and they gave us two blankets to keep us warm. I don't know who they were, and I never saw them again, but they appeared to be on the Lord's errand. I felt that the protection of God was with us on that fateful trip to California.

We finally arrived in Southern California and moved in with friends in the city of Santa Ana, where there was a thriving Cambodian community. A new chapter in our lives was beginning, but there would be many hard times ahead.

I finally found a community college in Santa Ana and six months later earned a nursing assistant certificate. While finishing the program, I served an internship with the respiratory department and became very interested in pursuing that degree. I enrolled in the respiratory program at Orange Coast College, attended from 1985 to 1987, and graduated with the respiratory certificate and an associate's degree. Later I would earn a bachelor's degree in organizational management/leadership from Ashford University in Iowa. Like my father always told me, education would be the key to my future.

In Santa Ana, I had a Cambodian friend who hassled me all the time for being Mormon. She said I was a two-headed snake—one head Buddhist Cambodian and the other head American Mormon. She couldn't understand why I would be a traitor to all our beliefs. I tried to explain what the Church meant to me, but she wouldn't listen. Her children did, though. She had four rebel teenagers, and they all became interested in the Church. They took the missionary lessons, mended their ways, and got baptized. Her daughter had to quit smoking to do it, but they all became great members. Her daughter even served a full-time mission. They became a powerful missionary force in their neighborhood and helped the missionaries teach and convert their whole block. My friend never joined.

During the school year, I continued to attend Church meetings and introduced the missionaries to hundreds of Cambodian people in the Santa Ana area. Within the next ten years, approximately seven hundred Cambodians from the "South Minnie" (the name of the street in Santa Ana where the Cambodians lived) area were introduced to the gospel and were baptized into The Church of Jesus Christ of Latter-day Saints. I spent many hours with the missionaries in the evenings to translate the discussions for the Cambodian investigators who couldn't speak English. I also had many opportunities to translate lessons during Sunday School and Relief Society classes at church, which met in the Irvine building. In the meantime, I continued to battle the odds. I had to deal with an abusive husband while raising two little children, going to school full time, and working part time on the school campus. I prayed night and day for the strength to go on and to provide a good life for my children.

I often asked myself how a tiny person like me should be required to bear all these hardships and responsibilities that I had carried since I was eighteen years old. I remember one Sunday, I met with Branch President Bollard and asked him why all the challenges and suffering were continuously inflicted upon me. President Bollard replied that the Lord loved me very much. He knew that I could handle all these challenges and that I would become stronger in the process. As I continued to have faith and pray, I began to see how the Lord was always with me. Looking back into the past, I know that the successes that I have found would not have been possible if I didn't have constant help from the Lord.

After working three years as a full-time respiratory therapist, I saved enough money for a down payment on a house in Riverside County. I was also able to raise my two children on my own and get out of an abusive marriage that I had endured for eleven years. At times I blame myself for the verbal and physical abuse that I and my children suffered at the hands of a cruel, inhumane father and husband. In the past, when I had limited resources, my options were also limited. I had no family or friends around to turn to for help. However, all the pain that I and the children had to bear motivated me to finish school, get a good job, and get my children out of that ugly situation. I succeeded in getting a divorce and became completely independent of my abusive husband in 1989. My children and I moved eight times during the past twenty-seven years in the United States. I finally settled in Brea, Orange County, California, after being married to my present husband, LaMar, in 1993.

LaMar and I were married in the San Diego Temple on July 24, 1993. The children, Soktheas (Scotty) and Charya, were later sealed to us in the Los Angeles Temple in 2001. Charya, my daughter, after attending BYU for one year, was also married in the San Diego California Temple in 2001, and my son, Scott, was married in the Washington D.C. Temple in 2009. As of now, the year 2010, my husband is semi-retired, and I am still working as a respiratory supervisor at St. Joseph Hospital in Orange, California. My son, Scott, a graduate from the United States Naval Academy in 2004, is now a lieutenant in the US Navy. Scott proved to be an excellent athlete at Brea Olinda High School, having earned nine varsity letters upon graduation. As a result of his football skills, he was recruited by the Naval Academy and played four years for them. My daughter, Charya, a graduate from George Mason University in Virginia, is now a news reporter in Maryland. Both Charya and Scott graduated from high school with honors and were recognized as athletes of the year. They learned how the Lord can help you succeed if you do all you can to prepare yourself along the way.

I was deeply moved every time "The Star Spangled Banner" was played at the beginning of each high school football game. It was the most wonderful feeling I ever felt to watch my son run the football on the field as his sister led cheers from the sidelines. The anthem represents the freedom and opportunity that I have tried so hard to obtain and that has blessed our lives so much.

Over and over, I have seen the Lord's mercy and protection. People can take away your homes and property. They can deprive you of food and clothing and shelter. They can ridicule you and spit on you. They can even kill your family and friends. But they cannot separate you from the Lord's love and kindness. I've been to the temple and performed the saving ordinances for family and friends killed in Cambodia. The Lord always triumphs over evil. I believe that after riding out the storm, you can always find the sunshine again. Challenges will present themselves in life, but with faith, all the bumpy roads will make you stronger. As you try your best to do your part, the Lord will take care of the rest. And that's most of it!

Sokcheat Stewart with her husband, LaMar (in middle), son, Scott, and his wife, Courtney (on left), and daughter, Charya, and her husband, Seth (on right).

VISETH VANN

My name is Viseth Vann. I was born in Phnom Penh, Cambodia, on June 1, 1972. Our family consisted of my mother, my father, myself, and three younger brothers. At that time, my family was upper class. Dad was a high-ranking military policeman, and Mom came from a very well-educated family of professors and politicians.

In 1975, the Khmer Rouge took over our country. They wanted to turn the entire country into a poor, agrarian society that they could then reshape and control. So they forced us all out of the city and sent us to villages. My mother's extended family members were all light-skinned, so the Khmer Rouge suspected them of being upper class and had them all killed. My mother was quite dark-skinned, so they didn't pay any attention to her. That was why she escaped execution. She was the only member of her family that survived. My dad was pretty good at storytelling. He made up lots of stories to tell the interrogators, so he convinced them he was an illiterate taxi driver. They believed him and let him live.

My folks took us to a small village where no one knew them and they could lie low about their upper-class, military past. It was the village where our grandmother lived. She was sort of the matriarch of the town and held a lot of influence, so the Khmer Rouge left her alone.

Our house was on stilts. The communists dragged our parents off to the fields to work all day, so we just had to fend for ourselves. The officials gave us one meal a day. It was a small bowl of rice water. We had to secretly hunt for any other food we could find. We were always hungry. So we would scavenge around all day looking for things to eat. We learned how to fish in the streams. My parents would return at night from working in the fields and would have cuts and bruises all over from where the supervisors had beaten them. But we were always happy to see them.

I loved my mother and appreciated the little time I had to spend with her. Mom would sometimes smuggle her lunch back to us to eat at night. One day my mother and I came across a corn field. We noticed there were no guards watching the field. As we started to pick some of the corn, a group of Khmer Rouge leaders approached us from behind. They took the corn away from us. They knocked me to the ground and then beat up my mother with sticks. They warned us never to do that again or worse would happen. Then they let us go. As we started to limp home, I took out two ears of corn I had in my pants. My mother wiped away the blood from her mouth and the tears from her eyes. She started to laugh at my joke and said what a clever boy I was. We ate the corn and enjoyed a forbidden pleasure together. From that day on, I was able to ignore all the Khmer Rouge's attempts to get us to hate our parents. I knew who my real allies were.

All I had to wear was one pair of pants. I had no shirts. When the pants got dirty, I'd go play in the stream to get them clean again. We really had nothing.

With our parents being hauled off to work in the fields, no one was around to see that we were in school. So my brothers and I spent most of the day playing and looking for food. We'd play kick the can and hide and seek. Then we'd go hunting for something to eat: bats, birds, snakes, and frogs—anything would do. We'd take our catch to our grandmother, and she would cook it up for us. She taught us to stay away from the Khmer Rouge when we could and to play dumb whenever they came around.

Before long, people started disappearing from the village. Parents of friends would not come back from the fields at night, so the kids would move in with us. Officials told them their parents had been sent to other towns to work, but eventually they would figure out that their parents had been killed. Everyone was so afraid of the Khmer Rouge that no one would risk talking about what they were doing. You couldn't even cry over lost loved ones or they would suspect you of rebelling against the system and take you away.

One day the town ran out of food to feed the people. So they decided to exterminate the entire village. They packed us all up and told us we were moving to a new town. They moved us to a ghost town near the Vietnamese border and left us there to do whatever we wanted for a while. That was so unlike the strict control they usually exercised over everyone that my parents figured out we were all going to be executed. At night, we could hear gunshots and planes flying overhead as the Vietnamese were attacking the Khmer Rouge. Of course, we had no idea who was attacking, but my mother would secretly pray every night that whoever was fighting them would win so the Khmer Rouge couldn't kill us.

After two or three weeks, our guards told us to have a party and eat all the food that was left. My parents figured out they were going to kill us all the next day. My mother prayed all night for our deliverance. We were Buddhists and didn't really know who we were supposed to pray to, so she prayed to our ancestors. But she had great faith that there was a power guiding our lives. The next day, instead of facing our guards, we found the Vietnamese had come in and taken over. We all celebrated having been spared.

My parents took us back to the capital city, Phnom Penh. We went to our old house and found it in ruins. The city was still pretty much empty. We waited around for a week or two, hoping my mother's family would come back to find us. No one came, so we worried that they had all been killed. My dad didn't want to stay there very long because the Vietnamese communists weren't much better than the Khmer Rouge. But my mother held onto the hope that some of her family might have survived and would try to return, so she convinced Father to stay awhile.

Dad was very bright and understood how things worked in Cambodia. He was able to scrounge up food and even started a little restaurant. We did okay for a while. But my dad was distrustful of the Vietnamese officials and started planning how he could get us all out of the country.

One day he packed us up and took us out of the city. On our journey into Thailand, we saw dead bodies everywhere. The Vietnamese and Khmer Rouge were still fighting. We had to dodge land mines along the way and sometimes would see people blown up by them right in front of us. At night, desperate people would run around and rob the other people fleeing like themselves. We were robbed twice and lost all the money my dad had saved to try to make the journey. There were checkpoints everywhere on the roads, and several times we were sure we were going to be caught and killed. But the Lord must have been watching over us, and we made it to the Thai border. So many others didn't make it.

My mom had hidden some jewelry that we intended to use to pay someone to get us across the border. But while they were trying to arrange it, we were captured by the Khmer Rouge. They forced us to help them fight the Vietnamese and kept us there for three months. But they lost their battle, and my dad finally found a truck driver to smuggle us across the border.

Getting into Thailand, we finally thought we would be free. But life was miserable in that refugee camp there. We had to stand in long lines waiting for our two small meals a day of rice water and dried fish. Once a day, a truck would come by with water. We just held out an old tin can and filled up. You had to ration what little they gave you. We lived in tiny shacks, and it was hot and miserable. We were there for five years waiting for someone to help us.

Dad grew desperate and began to try to get us out of that refugee camp at all costs. So he snuck back into Cambodia to look for relatives that could help us. He was caught and put in prison for three months. When they released him, he found it was harder to get back across the border into Thailand, and so he was stuck. We found out we had a relative who had made it to Texas and could sponsor us there. But we didn't want to abandon our father. Finally, he wrote us a letter telling us to make our way to the United States without him and then we could try to find a way to sponsor him later.

The Thai guards treated us very poorly. They would rob us, beat us, and do whatever they pleased with us, and there was no one to stop them. One time they came in and beat the entire camp because they thought someone had stolen something from them.

Local people from a nearby village would come up to the fence around the camp and try to sell us stuff. It was against the rules, but sometimes the guards would look the other way. Other times they would punish the refugees, which was dumb because we were starving and just wanted food. One time I found a penny and tried to buy a piece of fruit from a villager through the fence. All of a sudden he took off running, and I knew I was in trouble. Two guards caught me. They began to beat me. I remembered that I had been taught by older kids what to do if they started to beat me. So I bit my tongue until it started to bleed. Then I let the blood out slowly to look like I had internal bleeding. When they saw that, they let me go because they didn't want to kill any of us. It was sad how much we had to use deception just to survive. Sometimes the truth kills.

I was young, but that experience left a strong impression on me. For the first time in my life, I thought maybe it was a bad thing to be Cambodian. I lost hope for any possibilities for the future. Even my mother, who had been our one strength through all of this, began to get a little desperate. She was alone with her children, trying to help us survive through this hellish existence. We would have done anything to leave there—even go back to Cambodia.

The only positive thing that happened in the Thai refugee camp was that we met Christian missionaries. Dozens and dozens of people came through to teach us and to help us. They taught us a little about Christ, but mostly they just had compassion on us and tried to help provide for our needs. They were the only ones I remember who showed us any genuine kindness through those years of insanity we had to face.

Finally after five years, our request for asylum in the United States was granted. We had to lie to our relative in Texas. My mom said she was her first cousin in order to convince them to sponsor us. When we arrived at the airport, we were the wrong family! They were furious with us. But eventually they understood how desperate we were to come to the United States. They even helped my mom find a job. She got paid to pick up trash on the side of freeways.

My brothers and I started at school. They put us in classes with a lot of Hispanics that didn't understand much English either. Since we didn't speak English, we didn't understand a word that was said at first. But we didn't care. It was just wonderful to be at school, making friends, and feeling safe. My confidence started coming back. Our mother was working two or three jobs, so we had to fend for ourselves when we got home. We lived outside Houston in a small town with a lot of other Cambodians. There were a lot of rivers and swamps, so we felt like we were back in Cambodia. We did a lot of hunting and fishing again—anything to get more food.

For several years, we tried to make contact with my father, but never with any success. We heard that he had been killed by the Khmer Rouge, but we were never able to confirm that. We were helpless.

Finally, we moved from Texas to Long Beach. My mother opened a little seamstress shop and made a decent living for a while. Then a lot more former refugees arrived and did the same thing. Competition got to be too heavy, and the business wasn't profitable anymore. We survived on government assistance. Again my mother began to feel anxious for our welfare. She made a desperate move to find some way to care for us and married a man who said he would do just that.

It turned out to be the worst mistake of her life. He never worked or did anything to help our situation. And he ended up being very abusive. For four or five years, he would beat my brothers and me and sometimes beat our mother. Three other kids came along, and he was abusive to them as well. It wasn't until we grew large enough to protect ourselves and our mother that he stopped.

As horrible as all our experiences had been as refugees, it was not as bad as our life in an abusive relationship with our stepfather.

Eventually we made contact with my real father in Cambodia. He was never able to leave. He finally remarried as well and had more children. I've talked with him a few times on the phone. I'm happy he was able to move on with his life.

When I was in high school in Long Beach, we saw the Mormon missionaries often. They would knock on our door and try to share their message with us. We were never really interested, but my mother was always nice to them. She would invite them in and feed them. Eventually they started taking us to play basketball with them. They showed us the same kindness and compassion we experienced from other Christian missionaries in Thailand. The missionaries started taking us to Church to meet other LDS youth. I met a lot of friends in the Church and was impressed with their commitment to the gospel. So when the missionaries asked us to be baptized, I said yes. I didn't really have a testimony, but I liked being surrounded with people who had so much passion for living righteously.

My brothers and I didn't go to church regularly at first. It was my mother who was a firm believer and attender. She encouraged us and prayed for us. It was mostly the social aspects that appealed to me. I started going more, mainly to get friends. We played basketball and volleyball, and I felt accepted and valued at church. I felt the sincerity of the many missionaries who came through and relied on the strength of their testimonies to make up for my lack of conviction.

It wasn't until I went to college that I realized I had to really figure out what I believed in. I started hearing a lot of people attack the Church, and it frustrated me that I couldn't answer their questions. It seemed like these anti-Mormons I met knew more about my religion than I did. For a long time, I would take the questions they raised to the missionaries, looking for answers. They were always able to help me find appropriate responses, and I took comfort in discovering that the Church could stand up to attacks. But I began to thirst for a better understanding for myself. I took religion and philosophy classes in college and had my beliefs challenged. I compared Mormonism with what everyone else had to offer and decided our faith really did stand up to the challenges. I finally started reading the scriptures for myself and was amazed as I began finding my own answers. It was then that I realized that I did believe the gospel. At least I had discovered an intellectual testimony of the Church.

I was still angry for a long time about all the things I missed out on in life. I never had a childhood. I never had a father who loved me. I never had the support of an extended family to turn to. I didn't have a national identity I could relate with. Because I focused so much on what I was deprived of, I failed to recognize the beauties and opportunities of life all around me.

Then around ten years ago, I had an experience that changed my life. I was totally healthy, and then one day I came down with a virus that knocked me out. It drained all my strength and landed me in the hospital. Doctors tested me for cancer and for everything they could think of, but they couldn't discover what was wrong with me. Every day

I could feel my body getting weaker and weaker, and I began to fear for my life. I would close my eyes to sleep, wondering if that would be the time that I wouldn't open them again.

My ward really supported me through this experience. They visited me and tried to cheer me up. And they prayed for me. I received several priesthood blessings and was promised that I would recover. I prayed and asked the Lord to give me another chance to make something of my life. One day, just as mysteriously as it had hit me, the infection left. I was totally cured overnight and discharged from the hospital. The doctors never did figure out what was wrong with me. And they never figured out what cured me. They called it spontaneous remission. But I knew what happened. The Lord answered all those pleas on my behalf and fulfilled the promises made in his name in numerous priesthood blessings. He granted me a new lease on life.

My whole life started to change. I was able to let go of all the bitterness and hatred from my past. I was able to let go of the anger toward the Khmer Rouge and even more miraculously toward my abusive father. I gave up my career as a business manager and my pursuit of wealth and found something more meaningful to dedicate my life to. I went back to school and became a guidance counselor at a high school. I started seeing all the beauty and glorious design in the world around me. I started seeing the goodness in everyone I met. With the Lord's help, I've left my past behind me and am now dedicating myself to my family, the Church, and to helping young people find direction in their lives.

The memories of the Killing Fields still have a profound effect on my mother. She still suffers a lot from what the professionals call post-traumatic stress. I have often asked myself how she found the strength to go on in the face of so much opposition. Was it the hope of a better day, the welfare of her children, or just a determined will to live? Perhaps it was all of those combined with her great faith in God. She turned to him regularly to pull her through each new abuse and setback. She taught us that it was no shame to be poor as long as we were not poor in spirit. She taught us that with God, we would always have meaning and a reason to keep on living.

My mother continues to inspire me to this day. She inspires me to overcome every obstacle and to always be grateful for what I have. "For every mountain there is a miracle," as the saying goes. And my mother taught me to rely on those miracles. I have seen many in my life. Joseph Smith, a mere boy, overcame persecution, tar and feathering, and countless abuses to restore and defend the gospel of Jesus Christ. Now that gospel has spread to all the world. I've seen the children of the Killing Fields become pioneers in embracing the gospel and letting it change their lives. They've gone on missions, have married in the temple, and are now raising their children in the Church.

My wife, Monida, and our two little boys, Vincent and Alex, mean everything to me. Monida had to sacrifice her friends and so much more to join the Church, but she did it willingly because she knew she had found the truth. Together we are learning the redeeming doctrines of the gospel and are trying to live them. In the Church, we have found the support and motivation we need to continue our journey home to Heavenly Father. We have found great friendship and role models of sacrifice and service. We have found the perfect pattern for raising families. But most of all, we have found the reality of the Atonement of Jesus Christ that allows us to repent of our sins, to let go of the suffering and abuses of the past, and to be cleansed and perfected for the Lord's kingdom someday.

BORA SAO

My name is Bora Phuon Sao. I grew up in Battambang, Cambodia, with my parents and two sisters, Sokunna and Sukunnaoy. I had two other siblings who died as babies. Life was very simple for us. We had no electricity, no indoor plumbing, and no running water. We used wells that we dug ourselves for all our water. Bicycles and ox-drawn carts were the main modes of transportation for most of the people. It wasn't uncommon for people to ride elephants as well. Even today, when electricity is more common, a lot of people can't afford a refrigerator, so they have to shop for food every day. Most people even today don't have cars. They drive around on little mopeds or motor scooters. All the homes were built on stilts to protect from flooding.

The children walked to simple schools each day and learned English or French. Sometimes parents would send their children to live with the Buddhist priests for a month or two to teach them about life and philosophy. We lived simple lives, practiced Buddhist rituals, buried our dead in humble cemeteries, and built memorials for our ancestors.

Then the Khmer Rouge came to power and changed all that. We were sent to live in small villages outside of the capital. They were basically concentration camps. There was no respect for property or tradition or even human life and dignity. Everyone was just trying to survive.

Our parents were sent every day into the rice fields. All the children old enough were sent out to work as well. I was three, and my sister Sokunna was two, so we were left behind. We would just walk around all day and wait for our parents to come back from the fields late at night. There was no one to watch us and nothing to do. We had no idea what my parents were going through, but we just felt abandoned. It must have tormented our parents to leave us each day. But the Khmer Rouge were in charge of every aspect of our lives.

One of the things the Khmer Rouge tried to control tightly was the production and distribution of food. They would send guards around all the time door to door to make sure you had enough food to eat. But really they were checking to see if you had any food in your hut they could confiscate. No one was allowed anything more than what they gave you. If they found hidden food, they would physically beat you and sometimes even kill you. But the rice rations they gave us were never enough to survive on. So our father would go fishing and then hide the dried fish in our shed. We would huddle in there and eat together under the cover of night. We had to lie and steal all the time to survive. We caught frogs and rats and whatever else we could to eat under cover. One time I saw a small cucumber growing on a vine at the back of the cafeteria. A guard saw me and came after me. But I was so hungry, I took it anyway and ran. They chased me all over the camp, but I was able to outrun them and find a place to hide and eat my stolen treasure. I was lucky they didn't catch me or they would have beaten me or even worse. I was four years old. It was such a horrible way to live.

My mother got pregnant while the Khmer Rouge were in power. She had the baby, but it was more a source of sorrow than of joy. Mother was so malnourished that she couldn't produce milk for nursing. The baby died after a few days. Everyone knew it would, but it was still so hard. That was our life: mostly death and the threat of death.

My parents realized we were never going to survive under the Khmer Rouge, and so like so many others, they decided our best chance was to make it to a Thai refugee camp across the border. They saved up by secretly selling fish and bananas to neighbors until they had enough to pay for the guide. There were about thirty of us that left at the same time—ten or twelve families together. We just marched for days across the jungle. Our lives were in jeopardy every moment, but to me it was just an adventure. When we got close to the border, we had to stay frozen where we were during the day and crawl at night to avoid being shot by the Thai guards or the Khmer Rouge soldiers. There were land mines everywhere, and that made things even trickier. People had their legs blown off, and many were killed by stepping in the wrong place.

At one point, my aunt and I were moving right next to each other and were one foot away from crawling onto a land mine. But our guide saw us at the right time and told us to freeze. We did and missed the mine. The Lord was looking out for us or we would have been killed. It took us several weeks to get across the border.

Life at the refugee camps in Thailand was much better than life under the Khmer Rouge. The guards and police would rough us up a little and steal from us, but the Thai people were kind. And we had much better food to eat: dried fish, canned tuna, and chicken. It was a feast compared to our meager rations under the Khmer Rouge. They had school for us, and we studied English. We were able to practice our Buddhism again. We spent several years in three or four different camps.

The goal for everybody was to get a sponsor in the United States. We had tried for years without success. Finally my father bribed a camp official and got sponsorship papers for a family that was no longer at the camp. We were going to pretend we were them and use the papers to get into the States. They even dressed me up as a girl to pretend to be the family's daughter listed in the papers. But just as we were leaving under disguise as this other family, we received notice that our own petition for sponsorship had been accepted. Our aunt and uncle had found sponsors in Provo, Utah, and now had found sponsors for us. We were able to go as ourselves. I was ten years old.

We landed first in San Francisco and then connected to a flight to Salt Lake City. As we landed, the whole city was covered with something that looked like cotton. We had never seen snow before. None of us had a jacket, so we were all freezing. But we were so grateful to be there—wherever it was that we were! Our sponsor family lived in Provo. They took us in and saw to our every need. We went to school and started to live normal lives again. They invited us to church a few times, but they saw we were strong Buddhists and respected our beliefs. I remember going with them to Temple Square and feeling very peaceful—as if we were in a holy place.

We enjoyed our brief stay in Provo. But we had relatives in Long Beach, and they spent months persuading us to move there. They said the weather was more like what we were used to in Cambodia: warm, muggy, and no snow! They even sent us money to help make the trip. So after a year and a half, we bought a car, packed up our few things, thanked our sponsors, and drove to Long Beach in the summer of 1985.

It took all our money to pay for gas. We had no money for a motel, so we slept in the car. When we arrived at Long Beach, we stayed with my aunt for three months until my parents were able to save a little money to rent an apartment of our own. They both earned money at first by picking cherries in the fields. Eventually my dad got a job as a donut baker, and my mom started sewing and selling clothes out of our apartment.

Life was hard for us kids. I was twelve years old and enrolled in elementary school. I had to walk every day. There was a lot of ethnic conflicts between the blacks, the Hispanics, and the Cambodians. We'd get called names, picked on, and beaten up. By the time I got into Lakewood High School, the opposition was so bad that it was potentially deadly. The only way we felt we could survive was to join a Cambodian gang. The initiation into a gang was called getting "jumped in." Six or seven of the gang members made a circle around you. Then they were given thirty seconds to beat the tar out of you. After you survived that ordeal, you were officially in the gang. A lot of the gang members would show off their bravado and start things with other gangs, but I was just looking for protection. If gangbangers from other gangs would bother you, you just made the signs of your gang, and they would leave you alone. For me it was all about survival.

I had joined the gang for protection and security, but I learned the hard way how little they really had to offer. One day a group of us were hanging out on the street together. We saw a Mexican girl, and some of our gang started giving her a bad time. She threatened to go get her gang and let us have it. They challenged her to try it and laughed at her threats. Then she disappeared. A little while later, we were standing at a bus stop when suddenly everyone in our group took off running. I had my back to the street and didn't see what was happening. I turned around just in time to watch a large Cadillac pull up to the bus stop and almost a dozen Mexican gang members piled out along with the offended girl. She pointed angrily at me even though I hadn't said anything in the earlier encounter. And the furious gangsters quickly gathered around me and began discussing my fate. I knew I was done for, but something inside of me just told me to stand still and keep silent. They started taunting me, and I could tell their intent was revenge for the girl's tainted honor. They were going to beat me to a pulp or maybe worse. Without the protection of my gang members, who all flew off like cowards, I was sure I was a goner.

Then somewhat mysteriously a bus pulled up to the stop and opened its doors. No one got on or off. It just sat there with its door opened—as if it were calling to me. The gangsters had all completely ignored the arrival of the bus. But it was silently calling out to me as if it were a heavenly chariot sent for my rescue. I slowly and deliberately started to weave my way around the Mexican gang members in my path. None of them made a move to stop me or even touch me. It was as if suddenly I had become invisible to them. I calmly walked right past them all and stepped up on the bus. The door immediately closed, and the bus drove off, taking me to safety. There was a power higher than any gang influence looking out for me that day.

I never got involved with my gang much after that. I stayed as far away as I could. But occasionally I would do things with friends I met there. One day during my senior year of high school, some of them invited me to a large party. When we got there, it actually was a fund-raising dance for a church. My friends thought it was all too clean and boring, so they left early. But I liked the people there. I especially liked one of the dance organizers named Kim.

As soon as I saw Kim across the hallway, I pointed her out to my friends and said I was going to marry her some day. I had no idea what I was getting myself into. She was a Mormon. We talked and danced and had a good time. But as an organizer, she had a lot to do to keep the dance going. I stayed to the end and helped her clean up. But before I could offer her a ride home, she had slipped out another door and went home with a friend. I didn't get her phone number, so I thought I'd never see her again.

But three weeks later, I went with my family to El Dorado Park for a Cambodian New Year celebration. As we were crossing a small bridge, all of a sudden out of thousands and thousands of people, there she was, coming the other way across the bridge. We started talking again, and things just seemed to click with us. Before our walk in the park ended, I was telling her about my dreams of being successful in life and raising a family and so many other things we seemed to share common views on. She started taking me to church and introduced me to the missionaries.

My family was opposed to my joining the Mormons, so I took the lessons at Kim's house with her family. I quickly dumped all my old friends and easily adopted new ones at the branch I attended with Kim. It was an easy decision for me to be baptized. I was seventeen. My parents reluctantly accepted my decision at first. They even came to my baptism. My friends and family were there, and I knew I was making the right decision.

But when my parents saw all the activities and callings the Church gave me, they began to resent it. I was quickly called to be the mission leader and started spending a lot of time helping the full-time missionaries. My parents felt as though all my time was taken up by the Church and that I didn't have any time to help out at home anymore or to prepare for my future. Church members helped me see how they were right, so I started balancing my time better. That helped smooth things out with my parents a bit. I graduated from high school and went to Long Beach City College for two years.

It was through my calling as ward mission leader that I really discovered my testimony. Going door to door and sharing my new beliefs with others helped me realize that I really did believe what we were teaching. I could see the changes that had come into my life, and by sharing them with others, the Spirit witnessed to me over and over again that I was on the right path.

My family started seeing all the changes that came into my life as well. My sisters and several of my cousins began taking the missionary discussions and were all converted. Our parents decided that the Church was a good thing that had come into our lives and encouraged us in it even though they haven't joined yet themselves. My sister Sokunna married a returned missionary in the San Diego Temple.

The biggest obstacle I had to face was Kim's parents. I was Cambodian, and her family was Chinese. That cultural barrier was too big for them. They opposed us getting married. A successful Thai businessman Kim had never met asked her parents for her hand in marriage. They were excited about his prospects and encouraged her to accept. I felt that if that's how strongly her parents felt, and knowing they were looking out for her welfare, then I would slip out of the picture and let her marry him. But she assured me she didn't want the rich, successful man. She wanted me! It took us almost seven years, but finally we convinced her parents, and we were sealed in the Los Angeles Temple in 1997. Kneeling across the altar and looking in Kim's eyes, I knew it was worth the wait. Like Jacob working seven years to marry Rachel, my seven-year wait to marry Kim seemed like a tiny sacrifice.

I was raised a Buddhist. Like with most Cambodians, it was

a cultural thing for me. My parents taught me to pray to God even though as Buddhists we supposedly didn't believe in God. But I know that God was watching over my life from the beginning. Now as a member of The Church of Jesus Christ of Latter-day Saints, God is right in the center of my life. He has helped me let go of my past and forgive those who hurt me so much. I can see now that all through my life, he was there watching over me and shaping my destiny. With his help, I am building a family that I know can last forever. Nothing else really matters that much anymore.

Bora with his sister Sokunna, his parents, and his baby sister, Sukunnaoy, in Cambodia

KIMSIENG SAO

My name is Kimsieng Sao. I was born in Pursat, Cambodia, on March 11, 1973. I have no birth certificate. The only way my mom was sure of my birthday was that I was born on the day of the annual canoe competition. I was about three years old when the Khmer Rouge invaded Cambodia. Mostly, all I have are piecemeal flashbacks of my chaotic childhood. But I know they happened. I lived them.

Kimsieng (youngest) with her mom and siblings in Cambodia in 1974

My mother was a housewife. She made extra money by running a simple little library out of our house. She checked out used books to people for a small fee. My father was a carpenter and ran a small business. My earliest memory is flying with him somewhere in an airplane. My parents were educated and well off financially. Later that would make them prime targets for the communists.

My parents moved the family to Phnom Penh. There we lived on the second floor of a New York–style high rise. We were a happy, successful family—content in our little world. We were Buddhist, like everyone else. But our Buddhism was more of a cultural thing than a religious one. We celebrated the Buddhist holidays and fit in with our neighbors and family. And then the Khmer Rouge came to our city and nobody fit in anywhere.

My last memory before the war started was playing with my favorite toy: a pretend TV that had a dial to turn and make still pictures roll through the screen. Then all of a sudden, bombs started going off in the city as the communists attacked. One of my relatives snatched me off the floor, put me on his motorcycle, and drove me out of the city for protection. We were all supposed to gather in a designated spot. Not everybody made it.

The Khmer Rouge sent everyone to live in camps at the villages. They assigned guards, leaders, and supervisors at each camp. My mother kept me always near her side. For years she kept telling everyone that I was three years old so they wouldn't send me off to work in the fields. Fortunately, I was small, and she got away with it. My oldest sister, Kimky, was sent off by the communists to live in another camp nearby. But the rest of the family was there with us: my father, my other sister, Kimyong, and my brothers, PhicEl, PhicHo, PhicKaing, and PhicOr. I just don't remember them very much because they had to work in the fields all day, every day.

I remember living in a small village in a little hut. It was made out of dry coconut leaves and stood on long, tall stilts. When it rained, the water rose quickly, and the village flooded. Then you could pull the floor up higher on the stilts so the water would all pass underneath without disturbing the hut. But you'd have to watch out for little critters that would come with the water, like rats and snakes. I remember my grandmother—my dad's mom—would always wake up in her corner of the hut with a snake curled up beside her. They were harmless, so we'd catch them and eat them in a delicious soup.

It seemed like the main activity of each passing day was simply to stay alive, and that meant finding food. The communists gave us only rice water to live on. They called it soup, but it had ten times the amount of water you'd normally cook rice with. We'd meet in the cafeteria once each day for this feast, so we were always hungry. It was against the rules to have any other food, but we all did what we had to, to survive. Our near constant occupation was to find more food without being caught and potentially killed. There was a food storage facility near our little hut where they stored rice grain. Rats would come to eat the crumbs left after the food was gone. My dad made little traps out of boxes, caught the rats, and roasted them over a fire. They were the most delicious meat I had ever tasted. We often would catch red army ants as well. We just stir-fried them like rice and ate them plain. They were sour and juicy, but we paid a price in catching them. We always got stung bad, but they were worth it. Occasionally we ate crickets too. They were fried in a pan or roasted over a fire.

One day my oldest brother, PhicEl, took me out in a little field at one end of the camp and built a small fire. He broke up some coconut pieces, and we cooked them over the fire. I remember how tasty they were. Then he kissed me and sent me home. I never saw him again. My parents heard rumors that he took off with his friend to get away from the slavery of the camp. They were bright, educated young adults who thought they could outsmart the communists. We never heard from him again. We assumed that they found him and killed him. We always held to a small hope that perhaps he had survived. After we got to America, we made a flier and had it distributed around places we thought he might have gone to if he had escaped— just in case he survived. But of course, we never heard anything from him.

One time my mother found out that my oldest sister, Kimky, in the other camp didn't have much food to eat. So my mother and I walked to her camp to see if we could help her. I remember how long and silent of a journey it was. We had nothing to take her and had to beg for food ourselves just to make the journey. We stopped at a stranger's hut and asked if we could sleep on their hammock for the night outside their hut. It seems odd now, but I can remember how hungry I was and yet how peacefully I could fall asleep. I was so tired and felt the security of being next to my mother. That made up for everything. When we finally arrived at my sister's village, we had to sneak into the camp without anyone noticing we were from another camp. We managed to find her shelter. She was literally starving to death. We just had a little food we had gathered along the way to give her. My mother and sister cried quietly in each other's arms.

On another occasion back at our village, I remember my parents getting very scared and even frantic. Apparently, my older brother, PhicKaing, had finished his labor in the rice fields one day and decided to go fishing to try to find more food for the family. The guards caught him and took him into the village. They were going to punish him. My mother went to fetch his supervisor for help. His supervisor stood up for my brother and said he was a hard worker. He said that he had done his share of work and should be allowed to go find food. If it hadn't been for the compassion of that one man, my brother could have been executed. His crime? Trying to feed his family.

A lot of the work the Khmer Rouge gave the people to do was just to keep them busy so it was easier to control them. My older brothers didn't even live at our village. They were put in other nearby camps, and they could only come home on weekends to see the families. My parents said the leaders of our camp were reasonably nice compared to other camps. As long as you worked hard, they left you alone. In other camps, the people were not so lucky.

Our life under the Khmer Rouge consisted simply of survival. Rice water was all the communists gave us to live on. So with whatever free time we had, we went around looking for corn, fish, and clams to add to our diet. A river that ran by our hut proved to be very useful. We bathed in the river and did all our cleaning there. To get clean drinking water, we dug a hole in the muddy sand, and the water would seep into the hole and provided us cleaner water for drinking and cooking. The water buffaloes hung out in the river all day but seldom bothered us. You still had to be careful, though. If you hung out in the water for very long, the leeches would attach to you. I was attacked by them several times. They are small and flat as they attach on. They blow up like a balloon as they suck your blood, and then they get big and round and fall off.

One time I was playing in the river with my friends. All of a sudden, we saw a dead body floating down the river. We were scared but curious at the same time. So we ran along the river trying to look at it before the current took it away. It was the first time I saw a dead body. But it wasn't the last! I don't know why I didn't cry, but after that, I was afraid to walk anywhere at night.

The Khmer Rouge tried to execute anyone they could find who had been educated or wealthy or who was of the wrong ethnicity. My dad was a carpenter and had owned his own business. We were also of Chinese descent, which would have been enough to be executed, except we didn't look like traditional Chinese with the light skin and slanted eyes. The only way the communists could find things out was by interrogating people who might have known you. We were blessed that no one who knew us told them about our background. My mother was always worried for my father, though. Many times the authorities demanded he attend meetings that some folks didn't return from. They were interrogation meetings. But my father was a very kind and well-liked person. Everyone defended his character and said he was hardworking. So his life was saved.

My father spared me from hearing about all the horrors he saw. But he did share one. My cousin was appointed as a driver for some guards who were assigned to take two men away from the camp and execute them. His sister was assigned to be a witness and report back to the supervisors when the execution was complete. For some reason, the guards had only swords and were trying to cut off the heads of their victims. She had to watch as these two men fought back for their lives. But they didn't survive. Towards the end of the war, the Khmer Rouge were killing more and more of their own people while fighting the Vietnamese at the same time. They just started executing everyone for no reason. My uncle was executed by the Khmer Rouge. My dad was just blessed because a lot of people stood up for him. He said that if the war had lasted another week, he probably would have been killed too.

After the Vietnamese came in and kicked out the Khmer Rouge, we were left on our own. We weren't exactly free, but we were on our way. We still had to make our way back to our home in the city without being killed by the Khmer Rouge who were hiding in the countryside. There were thirty or forty of us following one person who seemed to know where we were going. You had to be very careful with every step because there were land mines everywhere. I remember my grandmother tried to walk but was so slow and unsure that two people had to carry her on a makeshift stretcher. You had to literally step in the exact footsteps of your guide or you could destroy yourself and others. We traveled a lot at night to avoid problems with anyone. Often nobody could talk. You could hear the leaves crunch under your feet. Occasionally my mother would even put her hand over my mouth to make certain I made no noises whatever. All I could hear was her heavy breathing. It was intense. Obviously, everyone was sure our lives were on the line. When our guide finally told us we were out of danger, everyone gave a hearty cheer. We ran up a hill to a road with lots and lots of people walking, making their way back home.

When we got to the city of Pursat, everything was in ruins. There was nothing to reclaim at our house. We had to find another place to rebuild. It was as if no one owned anything. You just found an abandoned house to move into, and it became yours. Life started up for us again. There was no money, so everyone had to barter. Often we used rice to buy things with. I started going to school again and learned to read and write. I learned to ride a bicycle and play in trees. We had food to eat and a life to enjoy again.

There were Vietnamese soldiers everywhere. They just became a part of everybody's life. The soldiers were friendly compared to the Khmer Rouge. We all learned to speak Vietnamese and spoke it on the streets and at the markets. One of them wanted to marry my sister Kimky, but my mom made sure that didn't happen. But the soldiers would visit a lot anyway and bring us treats. In a way, the Vietnamese saved us, but they had control of everything in our country for over a decade. The Cambodians don't like the Vietnamese now. There was too much bad blood between them.

My sister Kimky, got married. Her husband's family escaped Cambodia into Thailand and took her with them. From there they could apply as refugees to the United States. Kimky wrote to us to join them. So one day my parents just quietly and secretly packed up the family and headed for the border. They didn't even tell my grandmother we were leaving because they knew she would try to stop us. But they couldn't bear being separated from my sister and longed for the freedoms promised in America.

The journey to the Thai border was perilous. There were Vietnamese soldiers along the roads who offered some protection, but the Khmer Rouge were hiding everywhere, and they would rob or kill anyone. If they saw you in a big group, they would assume (rightly) that you were moving and would be carrying possessions, so they would certainly attack. We all broke up to walk into small, separate groups and tried to act like we were just strolling around. My mom and I walked together, but everyone else in the family went along by themselves. At one point, some guards stopped us and started interrogating my mother just when one of my sisters walked by. I was too young to understand what was going on, and when I saw her I yelled out to her, "Hey, we're over here!" So the guards pulled her over to interrogate her as well. I think my mom almost fainted at my innocent blunder. They stripped and searched my sister to see if she was hiding any money. My mom was afraid they would rape her. But they didn't. They searched her and then let her go. I really didn't understand what was going on, but my mother scolded me for putting us all at risk. She was trying to teach us how to survive.

The only things we managed to take across the border were a few old family photos, although my mother did learn one clever strategy for smuggling gold across. She took the little gold jewelry she had managed to save and melted it down. Next she shaped it into little pellets, like capsules. Then she swallowed them. She tried not to eat or drink much crossing the border. Two days later, after we made it across, everything came out in her feces. Her plan worked perfectly.

Somehow we made it to a Red Cross refugee camp in Thailand. They took care of us there and fed us. They even started teaching us English. I'm not sure how old I was. My mom told everyone I was five for over three years just to keep me near her. When we made it to the United States, she had to change our birthdays so we could get opportunities for education. My aunt had already made it to the States, so she was able to sponsor us. First they flew us to the Philippines and gave us more English lessons. I tagged along with my parents to their ESL classes and picked it up quickly, so I became a translator for the class. I think it was there in the Philippines that I remember seeing a refrigerator for the first time. It was like a little glimpse of the good life. We finally boarded a huge plane and made it to the United States. The first thing I remember seeing was a traffic light. It seemed so strange and so clever. I couldn't understand how it knew when it was safe for people to cross the street!

It was a tremendous blessing to me that I was so young through all of this. As long as I was near my mother, I was never afraid. I didn't understand the seriousness of our situation. My parents had to live in terror every day that they might be executed and we'd be left to defend ourselves. But as long as I had my parents, I felt safe.

Through all our trials, I believe the Lord was guiding and protecting our path. Our aunt's sponsor in Long Beach was a Mormon and a good one. By the time we arrived, our aunt had joined the Church too. She started taking us to meetings with her. The missionaries started visiting our house a lot and taught us many lessons. Growing up Buddhist had given me a cultural identity, but I had never learned anything about the religion. The missionaries taught us where we came from, why we are here, and where we are going when we die, and it all seemed to make sense. Our lives had a purpose—to love God and our fellow man and to create an eternal family. From a gospel perspective, all the horrible experiences we had faced were part of the Lord's plan. This life is merely a test, an opportunity to grow by overcoming obstacles. Soon our entire family was baptized. At our baptism, I was invited to bear my testimony. I felt so clean spiritually. Even though I was only eight, it really felt like a new beginning to me.

Going to church in 1982: (l to r) PhicKaing, Kimyong, Mom, Kimsieng, Dad, PhicHo, PhicOr

In primary, the first song I learned was "I Am a Child of God." It explained everything for me. I knew that there was a God and that he had sent me to parents kind and dear to help me through the immense trials of my young life. Later, in Young Women, I thrived on attending Mutual and Girls' Camp in the summer. My desire to learn and grow in the gospel just took off.

I grew up as a teenager in Long Beach surrounded by gangs. It was easy to get sucked up into the wrong crowd. But in our little Cambodian-speaking Park Branch, I had the chance to serve in so many callings, and I think that's what kept me out of trouble. I served in all the Young Women presidencies and in Primary, and I even learned music. I was the branch chorister and then learned to play the piano so I could play at church as well. I had so many opportunities in the Church to develop skills and talents. Later I thrived in the young single adult program. We played together, worked together, served together, fasted and prayed together, ate together, and struggled through the challenges of our lives together. The missionaries called to serve us in the branch were our role models, and we wanted to become just like them.

My first year in college, our young single adult group decided to have a fund-raiser and missionary activity. To celebrate Cambodian New Year, we sponsored a dance and invited people in the community to come and pay a small entrance fee. I helped plan, decorate, and carry it out. We were hoping to raise funds and introduce people to the Church at the same time. It worked!

A young man named Bora arrived with a group of friends who were all in a gang. But he was dressed differently and acted differently. I met him, and he asked me to dance. His friends quickly realized that our dance wasn't going to be exciting enough for them, and they left. But Bora stayed. We danced a lot, and I enjoyed his company. A few weeks later, we met again at a community event at the park, and he asked for my phone number. I told him we could hang out, but he would have to choose between his friends or mine. He chose mine! Before long, he took the missionary lessons and joined the Church. His two sisters joined as well. Five years later, we got married in the Los Angeles Temple in 1997. His sister married a returned missionary in the temple as well.

The key to happiness in life is faith and family. We're trying to raise our children with both their American and Cambodian heritages. Our children speak English, Cambodian, and Chinese. We talk with them all the time about our experiences and try to help them to be grateful for the abundance we enjoy here. We're trying to raise them to want to go to the temple someday themselves.

In high school, my brothers were challenged by scientific theories. One of them decided he wanted to be a doctor and began to adopt a secular, scientific worldview. He would debate with me all the time about God and the Big Bang Theory. He was a lot smarter than me and always seemed to win our discussions. I would cry for hours afterward.

Later he married out of the Church and pursued his interests in medicine. But after I got married, our families stayed connected. We would spend a lot of time together. My sister-in-law started becoming more and more interested in the Church. We went on vacation together to Big Bear and ended up staying all day in the cabin talking religion. Now my brother and sister-in-law are attending Church and meeting with the missionaries.

My other brother married in the temple and is raising his family in the Church. He's doing a lot of genealogy and temple work for our family and trying hard to bring our extended family together. A lot of our relatives who weren't killed are still in Cambodia, so it's hard to contact them, but we're trying.

There are times when the challenges of life or the memories of the past can get me down. But attending Church, listening to general conference, and doing prayer and scripture study always get me back on track. I've never really had to deal too much with the anger, bitterness, or hatred that other Cambodian refugees have had to struggle with. I guess the Lord has just blessed me with a positive attitude. The blessings I enjoy now as an American, a Mormon, a wife, and a mother have all come to me because of our experiences that drove us from Cambodia. I know the Lord has had a plan for our lives, so I have no regrets.

I have no doubt that there is an unseen power that shapes the destiny of our lives. I see the love of Heavenly Father and Jesus in everything around me. Since the day I was born, Heavenly Father gave me parents to lead me, guide me, and walk beside me. As bizarre and chaotic as my childhood was, I never knew it. As I walked in the protective shadow of my mother, my world was safe and secure, and my faith in God was intact. He put strangers in our path to guide us through the darkest times into the light and safety. He gave me leaders who helped to shape my life and my desires and groomed me into a leader myself. He took a scared, displaced little girl out of the Killing Fields of Cambodia and put me safely on the gospel path headed back to my heavenly home. I was lost but now I'm found—a willing and grateful sheep in the Savior's sheepfold. Praise be to the Lord forever and ever!

Kimsieng in 2010 with her husband, Bora, and children (l to r): Landen, Mason, and Serena

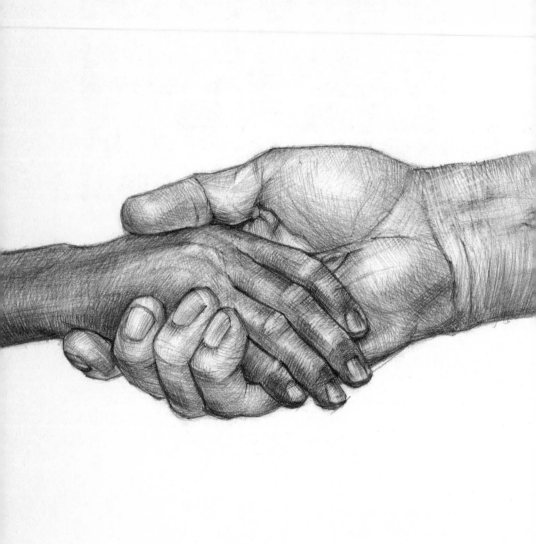

CHENDA TIRAPHATNA

I don't know when I was born. My mother never got a birth certificate, and our lives were a bit chaotic in Cambodia. My mom's best guess is that I was born in April 1971. Our family consisted of my parents, my four brothers, and me. From my earliest memory, we had to work hard to survive. My parents would send us out on the streets to sell whatever we could.

My very earliest memory is from a day my brother and I were playing under our hut. All the homes were built on stilts to help them survive the flood waters. And that left a small region under the house where kids could play. We were just playing and digging as kids do, when we unburied a human skeleton. It horrified me. I always felt afterward like we lived in a haunted house, and I was terrified of it. It turned out to be a foreshadowing of much worse things to come.

When the Khmer Rouge started taking over, I remember a lot of bombing. We were buying candy and selling it on the streets to try to get a little money to buy more rice with. Meanwhile bombs were going off around us, but they just became part of our day. The river would flow with dead fish everywhere, killed from all the bombing. But we still had to survive, and that meant selling our candy.

Our life consisted mainly of selling things and finding food. A big pot of rice water would consist of maybe two or three tablespoons of rice. So we would gather whatever vegetables we could find to mix in with it. Then we would go scrounge up anything else to supplement our diet. We'd eat tadpoles and crickets and crabs and just about anything we could find. But most of the time, we were on the verge of starving to death.

My little brother got sick. He had thresh on his tongue, diarrhea, and a host of other problems. We had no medicines, and the Khmer Rouge had eliminated all the hospitals, so we had no place to take him. He was less than two years old, and we just had to watch him waste away and die. It devastated my parents, of course, but they had no other choice but to carry on and try to help the rest of us survive.

The Khmer Rouge rounded us all up and moved us into a camp. We weren't there very long, though. My father had served in the military before the communist takeover, and they were killing off anyone from the old military. It didn't take them long to figure out my father's background. One day they summoned him with our entire family to attend an orientation meeting that night. But our friends all warned us not to go. People at those "meetings" were just executed. My parents knew we had to get out of that camp that very night. They would have killed our entire family.

There were mercenaries who would smuggle you out of camp, through the jungle, and to the Thai border to escape the country if you could pay their price. Somehow my parents scraped up enough to get us out. We joined a group that left that night for the border. There were hundreds of other people scattered all throughout the jungle, trying to get away like us. We had around thirty or forty people in our group and were totally at the mercy of our guides. There was a little girl in one of the families who was mentally retarded. The guides took her out behind some trees and shot her through the head. They came back and explained that she might have given us all away to the Khmer Rouge by making too much noise and so had to be sacrificed for the good of the group. There was nothing her parents could do but accept it and go on with these awful men.

While we were journeying to Thailand, my brother and I reached a spot in our path where there were some branches and leaves piled up. Just as my brother was stepping onto the spot, we heard a voice say, "Don't step there!" We turned to see who it was and saw an old man sitting under a tree right next to the spot. He said, "There's a bomb under there." It was a land mine and would have probably blown us both up. Whether he was an angel or just an old man resting in the shade, looking back now I can see that Heavenly Father was truly leading us to the promised land.

When we got to the Thai border, we had to escape into the refugee camp. There were Thai guards everywhere trying to keep us out. We waited for the cover of night and then ran quietly between the guards. My dad pulled up some barbed wire and pushed me under the fence. Some of the people with us didn't make it.

Once we were established in the refugee camp, we went to work doing what we did best—selling stuff. It was against the rules for the refugees to sell anything, but that didn't stop us. My dad would send us outside the camp to gather up all the vegetables we could find. Then we would sneak back with the food and sell our "crops" to other refugees or to the Thai people. But the guards would beat you severely if they caught you. One time I had two guards coming after me, intent on teaching me a lesson. I ran and hid in one of the common bathroom huts. There was a long ditch that was used as a common toilet but looked deep enough to hide in, so I jumped in there. I prayed and prayed that no one would find me, and miraculously they didn't. They finally gave up looking for me and went their way. Once again the Lord was looking after me and protecting me.

One time I grew very sick. My mother was desperate to get me help because she could see I was going to die otherwise. She took me to see a nurse who was helping other refugees. I was so malnourished that I had shriveled up into just a mere skeleton. The nurse searched and searched to find a vein to stick an IV into me but without success. My mom prayed that the nurse would find a vein somewhere that would work. Finally, she found one on my ankle. She was able to stick it in and get me the life-saving nutrients I needed. To this day, I have a scar on my ankle where she pricked me. It's a symbol to me of my Heavenly Father's love.

For every family and individual in the refugee camp, the goal was to find a sponsor in the States. Somehow my dad knew a man living in Australia that went to work finding us help. He found a Baptist church in Jacksonville, Florida, that agreed to become our sponsors. But while we were all waiting for the paperwork to get approved, the officials sent us to Indonesia for processing. We had to wait there in a little camp for almost a year before the States would finally approve our immigration. By then my parents had separated. My dad left us for another woman. But my mom carried on valiantly without him to make sure we made it to the States.

In the camp in Indonesia, once again my mom put my brother and me to work finding stuff we could sell. She sent us up the mountainside to look for wild vegetables and coconuts. Then we would hike over rivers and valleys to the city ports by the ocean to trade for chickens and canned meat. We'd then hike back to the camp and sell the meat for a lot of money, since there was so little meat available in the camp.

Finally we got approved to travel to Florida and join our sponsors. They were all so kind and helpful and got us on our feet. But we were eager to be on our own. So when an opportunity arose to travel to Oregon to join in a fruit harvest, my mom took it. We were off to Oregon to pick strawberries.

One day the sister missionaries knocked on our door there in Oregon. They both had such a good sense of humor that we wanted to listen to them. They taught us that life had a purpose, and their message brought peace into our home. The people at Church were kind and embracing. We could just tell they had what we needed to move ahead in our lives. We were baptized when I was twelve years old. I probably didn't have a strong spiritual testimony of the gospel yet, but I knew that what we were doing was right. It was through attending the Young Women program and seminary over the next several years that I really discovered my testimony. I would need that personal foundation because eventually my mother and siblings stopped attending and I had to participate on my own.

By the time we were baptized, my dad had moved to Southern California. He made a living by picking through trash and pulling out items to recycle. Even though my dad had hurt my mom, she wanted us to live closer so we could have a relationship with him. So we moved to Long Beach. My mom got a job delivering newspapers. I would help her every morning before school. I grew up and graduated from high school there in Long Beach.

One day, in the young adult gospel doctrine class, I met a returned missionary named Jet. He seemed to me to be kind of a jokester, so I didn't take him seriously. But I guess he took me seriously. He got my name and phone number off an attendance role they had passed around the class, and he gave me a call.

Jet grew up in a Buddhist family from Thailand. They were living in South Gate, California, when he met the missionaries as a teenager. Jet decided he wanted to get baptized and go on a mission. His parents

were totally opposed to the idea. But they made him a deal. If he would become a Buddhist monk for six months, then afterward they would give their permission for him to do whatever he wanted in the LDS Church. So he became a monk to please his parents. They had hoped the monks would convert him to Buddhism, but the experience only solidified his testimony. Six months later, he was baptized, and a year later left on his mission to Boston, Massachusetts.

In Boston, Jet had the chance to work with a lot of Cambodians and began to learn to speak Khmer, the Cambodian language. When he got off his mission and returned to California, he decided to attend a Cambodian-speaking ward to look for a wife. He picked me! We were married in the LA temple. No one from either of our families could attend, which saddened us greatly. But we had ward members there to support us, and we knew what we were doing would last forever. So it was worth it.

I've always known that the Lord has been looking out for me. He spared my life so many times getting out of Cambodia. But the greatest miracle of all was bringing Jet into my life. He is Thai, and I am Cambodian. Our people were traditional enemies. Neither of our families really supported our marriage. But the Lord did, and that has made all the difference in our lives. Now we have five beautiful children—Chendara, Marcie, Robert, and the twins, Jacob and Jared. Everywhere we have moved, the wards we've lived in have been supportive and have helped us raise our children in righteousness. I am filled with so much gratitude for a loving Heavenly Father who has made all of this possible for us.

The Tiraphatnas: (left to right) Jacob, Chendara, Marcie, Robert, Jared, (in back) Jet, Chenda

KIMBERLY SANG VANFLEET

I grew up in a small town in northeastern Cambodia with my parents
and my three brothers. We don't have any records, but I think I was
born around 1960. When I was five years old, my father had an arranged
second marriage to the daughter of his friend as payment for a debt he
had to my father. This led to my mother divorcing him. My father was
in the military when the Khmer Rouge came to power in 1975.

When the Khmer Rouge took over, they split up the families. I was
sent to a camp with other teenagers like myself. They gave me a daily
quota of what I had to pick in the rice paddies, but I was so weak from
malnutrition that I could never meet their quota. So they punished me

by leaving me in the fields to sleep. They made me eat my one bowl a day of rice water out there. I was stuck in the watery rice paddies twenty-four hours a day for most of the five years the communists were in power. I was dying of malaria and malnutrition and asked to see my mother one last time before I died. They said I was faking and sent me back. I didn't get to see my mother at all those five years.

Because I was light-skinned, they looked for any way they could to justify killing me. Most of the time it was through starvation and over-working. Sometimes, though, they actively tried to kill me. They would tell me to go work at another camp and then were planning on killing me for attempting to escape, but I always figured out what they were doing and avoided their traps. Some of my friends were not so lucky. I watched them kill my cousin right in front of me. They tied her body up tightly like a package and then hit her on the back of the head with a stick. I watched them force a friend of mine to dig her own grave and then they hit her on the back of the neck with a heavy stick to kill her. She fell into the hole she dug and then they buried her. That way they saved bullets. But for some reason the Lord kept protecting me.

My cousin tried to escape to Thailand. But the Khmer Rouge caught him and brought him back to camp. They shot him and then killed his entire family as an example to others. They also brutally tortured and murdered my aunt. They stabbed and cut into her body as she screamed, and then they buried her alive. My mom had a breakdown and almost went insane. The only thing we could do was to suffer it all in silence. If you complained or even cried, they would shut you up by execution.

The Khmer Rouge soldiers were mostly ignorant children from rural communities. They were as young as ten years old, and few were over twenty. They were simply brainwashed by the communist leaders to accept that their parents were the enemy and had to be controlled or killed.

Because my father had served in the military, he knew the Khmer Rouge would eventually figure that out and kill him. He had a chance to escape, but he knew if he did, they would have killed all of his family left behind. So he stayed to face his fate. My father's niece was a Khmer Rouge leader, and she told them where they could find my father. So they took him off to an interrogation room. He was old and sick and dying of starvation. They beat him and demanded that he inform on others. But he refused to tell them anything. They finally took him to the home of one of the leaders, where he was forced to dig his own grave. They then beat him to death. Two of my brothers were dragged off to serve in the army to fight against the Khmer Rouge. The eldest, Eang, survived the war and returned to his family. The next one, Ung, was killed by the Khmer Rouge. He was only nineteen.

For my mom, my younger brother, and me it became clear that if we stayed in the Khmer Rouge camps, we would all die—by either starvation or execution. Our only chance of survival was to try to escape to the border and cross into Thailand to a refugee camp. My mother had no money to pay the guides but somehow persuaded them to take us anyway. While the Khmer Rouge were fighting with the Vietnamese, both my brother and I were able to leave our camp and make it back to where our mother was. So in November of 1979, we joined a group of about sixty people headed for the border.

The Khmer Rouge knew we were all trying to escape into Thailand, so they covered the entire jungle with land mines. They hung grenades from trees at the height of a person. They dug pits, filled them with sharpened bamboo sticks tipped in poison, and covered them with leaves. They didn't care who they killed or how—their one goal was to control everything. So we had to walk in single file lines, following the guides who knew how to spot the bombs. We had to avoid the Khmer Rouge soldiers, the Vietnamese soldiers who were fighting them by this time, and the Thai guards who didn't want us coming into their country. Fortunately, we were in a camp close to the border, so it only took us two nights to get there.

But we had no food or water. I saw a watering hole where no one was drinking. As I got close, I saw several dead bodies in it. But I was literally dying of thirst. I closed my eyes and drank. The water was putrid and made me sick. But it kept me alive. I stumbled upon a mango tree that no one was eating from. It was surrounded by dead bodies. The Khmer Rouge had placed land mines around the tree, knowing that starving refugees would flock there and be killed. I made my way carefully around the bodies and the remaining mines and took as much mango fruit I could carry back to my family.

In the dark of the night, I stepped on a land mine and should have been blown to bits. But miraculously the bomb didn't detonate. A former navy man saw me and told me to freeze. With my foot still on the bomb, he disabled it and saved my life.

Now to find a way across the border. The camps were all full and weren't accepting any new refugees. While we waited there, several of our group were raped by the Thai guards. My cousin's friend was raped. The guards would promise protection, round up a bunch of refugees in trucks, and then drive them all back to the Khmer Rouge camps, where they would be executed for trying to escape. Your one hope was if you had an American volunteer in your truck, then the guards would let that truck through. Some guards caught us and took us to a jail for three days. All the time I was praying blindly to whatever higher powers might be watching us that we could somehow make it across the border. When they finally loaded us into our truck, we were blessed. We had an American.

But our ordeal was far from over. The refugee camp we finally made it to was called Boredam. It was way overcrowded, and we often slept on the ground. Sometimes we slept in tents. But we had nothing—not even blankets. My brother and I used pieces of our ragged clothing to lay over our mom at night to try to keep her warm. The Thai guards took everything we had. They beat us for the smallest infraction of the rules. The only difference sometimes between them and the Khmer Rouge was that they usually stopped short of killing anyone. But they still humiliated and even raped us. My cousin was raped. We stayed there for about six months. Since most refugees had to stay there for three to five years, we felt blessed. For some reason, we were selected by a millionaire in San Francisco who decided to sponsor us. He sent us money through an agency to fly us to California. We had our ticket to freedom!

Apparently our sponsor wasn't really that interested in us. We never met him, but we were grateful just to have a new chance in a free land. After three months, we discovered we had a cousin living in Oakland, so we moved there. There's a power that comes in living near relatives. I found a job as a dental assistant and began learning English on my own so I could get along in this culture.

Every day going to and from work, I would see the Mormon missionaries out sharing their message with folks. They were so young and seemed so sincere. I felt drawn to them. They would greet me in the street and talk with me occasionally. One time they asked if I knew anything about the LDS Church. I replied that I was a Buddhist and didn't know anything about their church. They asked if they could come over and share their message with my family. I knew my brother really needed help. To drown out the pain of our past, he had turned to drinking. In the end, he refused to give up his drinking for the hope the elders brought us. But I enthusiastically embraced this new faith. I found all the answers I had been looking for to make sense of my troubled life. I could feel the truth of the doctrines the elders taught us. As I read the Book of Mormon, I felt the Spirit and knew it was true. I was baptized on a glorious day in the summer of 1981. As I came out of the water, I really did feel like a new life was beginning. The anguish I had suffered over my brother left. I felt clean and fresh, excited, and ready to go to work to help make the world a better place. As far as I know, I was one of the first Cambodians to join the Church in Oakland.

I immediately started serving with the missionaries. I would translate for them several times a week. This went on for five years while I continued to work as a dental assistant. One day, my brother failed to come home after partying all night with his friends. The stress on our little family was enormous. I was so worried about my brother and my mother, so I prayed with all my heart about what I should do. The answer came strongly from the Holy Ghost—I should go on a mission!

I received my mission call to Independence, Missouri, in 1985. It was signed by President Spencer W. Kimball. As far as I know, I was one of the first Cambodians to serve a mission. A senior missionary couple, the Johnsons from Spanish Fork, serving there in Oakland, encouraged me and helped me to get into the field. They wrote to me off and on my whole mission and became the moral support I needed. It was my mission that really strengthened my testimony as I saw the gospel change people's lives. It taught me humility and love for people and helped me let go of most of the bitterness of my past. I think I really learned a bit of what the Savior's life was all about—serving and teaching people even when many of them returned only hate and rejection.

I spent most of my mission in Wichita, Kansas, working with Asian refugees. We had a lot of success and saw a lot of converts to the Church. These were people much like me—broken off from their past and searching for direction to guide them in a new life. They found it in the restored gospel.

As productive as my mission was, I struggled a lot personally with concerns over my family. My mom had joined the Church three years after I did, but she really did not want me to go on a mission. While

I was serving, my mother decided to leave the Church and go back to Buddhism. Her friends convinced her that I had abandoned her by leaving on a mission, so she sort of disowned me. After finishing my service, I went back to California and tried to patch things up with my mom, but she didn't respond to any of my efforts. The combination of my mom's rejection and my brother's alcoholism was enough to drive me to seek a friendlier place to live. A former missionary companion lived in Tooele, Utah, and invited me out there, so a new adventure began as I went in search of the promised land.

I met up with a handsome returned missionary who I had worked with in Wichita. David Vanfleet and I were sealed in the Salt Lake Temple in 1987. David graduated from BYU in 1992, and we moved to Orange County in Southern California to work for Electronic Data Systems. While we were there, we had the blessing of attending the Park Branch in Long Beach. We were there until the year 2000, when we moved to Cedar City, Utah, and are raising four children here. We are trying to help them see themselves as both Cambodian and American. I tell them the stories of the war and what I learned. They tell me stories of being modern American teenagers. Sometimes their life seems as scary as mine!

Today our son is serving a mission in Cambodia. He is surrounded by poverty and hopelessness but is filled with gratitude for what we have in the United States. He has even had some success in helping people join the Church and start better lives for themselves. The gospel really does work to make people happier.

During my captivity in the Khmer Rouge camps, I would wake up every morning, look at the sky, and ask the universe, "Am I going to die today or am I going to live?" Every day that was the question. It terrified me to think of dying. My Buddhist faith didn't answer my questions about an afterlife. I had no hope of anything better on the other side. I was afraid death would end all my chances of happiness. I sincerely doubted that there was a place on earth where people could live free and happy lives. Most of my friends and relatives died in the camps. Even when we finally escaped, many of the people died along the journey or were killed by the guards when we got to the border. For some reason known only to the Lord, he chose me to live through all this and make it here. He introduced me to his Church and taught me about what happens after we die. Now I know what this life is all about as well. It's about creating and nurturing families. I believe that families really can be together forever.

Even with the understanding of the gospel perspective and the healing power of the Atonement, it continues to be a long, hard process to be able to forgive those who have hurt us so much. I know that they were mostly children who had been brainwashed into doing what they did and that they would have been killed too if they had disobeyed their superiors. But it is still a daily exercise to try and stamp out all the bitter memories and the resentment that comes with them.

To this day, there are a lot of former Khmer Rouge soldiers living in the United States. I've met some of them. I'm sure some have genuinely tried to change from what they were during the war to something better. But some are simply hiding from their past and pretending they weren't a part of it. I met a few of them in Long Beach. Some had even joined the Church and attended the same ward we did. I can't fully describe the anguish it put me through to have to interact with them as "brothers and sisters." But somehow the Lord helped me through that. I was able to let my anger go enough to allow the Lord to be their final judge. I learned to pray that he would help them change. I learned to pray for the Lord to change me and help me let go of the past.

I met former Khmer Rouge members on my mission in Kansas. Some of them actually opened their doors to us and embraced the gospel message we brought them. It would move me to tears to watch them accept the gospel and start a new life. I knew they were my former enemies, but Christ taught us to love our enemies. There was no better test of this for me than learning to rejoice in their conversions. I tried to say in my heart, "Forgive them, Father, for they knew not what they did." Even though some of them were not sincere and were still just trying to hide from and cover up their past, I tried to simply give them the benefit of the doubt and rejoice with all of them. My hope is that they will all be able to turn their lives around and make something good out of the life they have left. I am so grateful that the United States gave me a second chance on life. Now I have to give them a second chance on life as well.

I try to imagine that someday I will be able to go to the celestial kingdom, and I hope at that day that I will be able to greet my former enemies as true brothers and sisters. I know that Christ really can heal the breach between us and make us whole in his love. I am filled with gratitude beyond measure for my membership in his Church, my understanding of his doctrine, and my hope of redemption in his mercy. The Church doesn't just help us deal with the tragedies of life. It's true too. This really is all part of a divine plan that we accepted before ever coming here. My hope now is that I will be faithful to the end and pass my remaining tests of mortality so that I can enjoy my family for all eternity.

The Vanfleets: (back) Andy, Jessica, Vanessa, and Ashley, (front) David and Kim

SAROTH YAP

My name is Saroth Yap. I was born in Battambang in 1945. The older women in the village delivered the babies. I was the fifth of ten children—all born at home. We lived in a large house with nine rooms. I had to babysit the younger children during the day so my parents could work. Then I went to night school in the evening. As a child, my favorite game was hopscotch. Our only pet was a stray cat my dad used to feed.

I applied to be a nurse, and that's what I wanted to do with my life, but my parents took me out of school so I could help with the family sewing business. When I was in my early twenties, a man came to my parents and asked for my hand in marriage. I had never met him before in my life, but out of respect for my parents, I accepted his offer and got married. The day after we got married, he took me to his village where he lived and worked. I never saw my parents again. They died before I could return and visit. Life was hard for us in Cambodia. But nothing like how hard it was going to become under communist rule.

I was thirty years old and married with children when the Khmer Rouge came to power. My husband was a soldier in Lon Nol's army. So when the Khmer Rouge took over, they kept a close eye on us. They put us to work like everyone else. I had to make thatch roofs for huts, work in the rice fields, and do a lot of sewing. They also used me for making food to feed the village. All we had to eat in a day was one bowl of rice water. It was slave labor. They didn't have enough huts to house the people, so most of us slept outside on leaves for beds. Lots of people died. My brother, sister-in-law, and their five children were in a nearby camp. Somehow they got word to me that they were suffering terribly from exposure. There were no blankets and no warm clothes. I kept asking for permission to go help them. Finally, the officials in my camp let me go see what I could do. By the time I got there, my brother, his wife, and three of their children had died. My other two nephews died in my arms. I, myself, was so weak that I could feel the life draining from me. My husband had to force feed me some coconut and vegetables to keep me alive.

I recovered, and they sent me back to work in the fields. One time, as we were being sent out in the early morning, I saw a pregnant woman who said it was time for her delivery. I stayed behind to help her have the baby. When the officials found out I had missed my work assignment to help her, they interrogated me. They said that everyone had to look out for themselves. They yelled and yelled at me and threatened me with my life if I didn't conform to their rules. Three weeks later, the baby died. The mother wasn't healthy enough to produce breast milk, and there was nothing else to feed the baby.

They sent us from camp to camp, literally working us to death. When you got too weak to function, they would just send you to another camp. Sometimes they would uproot an entire camp and send us off to another village. By rotating us around, no one could band together to resist. Also, since you could only take what you could carry, no one could accumulate anything. They didn't even give us soap to wash with. Anyone who was too weak to travel and didn't have anyone to carry them was just left behind to die. They wanted us to die of starvation, exposure, or disease because then they wouldn't have to take care of us anymore. As we were being driven around, I would see old people abandoned and left to die. I would secretly give them water as I passed by, hoping that someone would do the same for my parents if they could. If the Khmer Rouge saw you helping anyone, they would punish you.

My younger brother was in another camp. He got fed up with the conditions and started to complain to his friends about their circumstances and their treatment. But some officials overheard his complaining. They had no toleration for that sort of thing. They took him to a place of interrogation and executed him on the spot. His friends witnessed it all and later came to my camp to tell me what happened. The Khmer Rouge were ruthless.

Every day there were people dying in the camp. Probably on average there were ten or more. Often they would use my husband to help dig graves. He would be the only one with the energy left to do anything. But there were so many to bury that they didn't have time to dig the holes very deep. So at night the wolves would come into camp to dig up and devour the bodies. Every night we slept in fear of the wolves.

They were always taking my husband in for interrogation. We lived in fear of being executed at any time. We lasted for about a year. Somehow my husband was very good at dodging their questions. With God's help, he survived. I got pregnant, and suddenly we felt responsible to protect our future family. Also, we could tell that they were getting more and more intense with their questioning and were likely going to kill my husband before too long. The Khmer Rouge had taken my husband into prison for five days for interrogation. While he was there, he witnessed a brutal murder. One of the communists had fallen in love with a Cambodian woman and wanted to marry her. She flatly refused him. He had her taken into prison and tortured. She was brutally raped and then killed with a sharpened bamboo stick. My husband decided that we simply had to get away from these people at all costs.

So we finally made our escape to Thailand. After leaving the village, we went for several days without food. We were starving to death. I said a desperate prayer, pleading with God to save us. I told him that if he had any purpose for our lives, he would have to feed us because we were so weak we could do nothing for ourselves. I told God that I would rather be eaten by a wild animal than killed by the Khmer Rouge or starve to death in the jungle.

After I finished praying, I looked up and was startled to see a full-grown tiger staring at us. But his eyes seemed gentle and inviting. Then he turned and slowly walked away. We felt compelled to follow it. And then this tiger led us to a bush with some fruit on it. It was sort of a Cambodian cranberry. We ate it and were able to survive. Then the tiger peacefully walked away. He saved our lives. He must have been sent by God. I know the story sounds crazy, but we were there and experienced it for ourselves.

We wandered through the jungle for months. There were no roads to Thailand. And of course we didn't have any maps. All we knew was that Thailand lay to the west of us. We could only travel at night most of the time because we were so afraid of being caught. But we didn't know how to read the stars for direction. So we would feel the trees for warmth to figure out where the sun had been shining on them. That was how we knew which direction to go.

We crossed mountains and rivers. At one point we jumped off a waterfall because we could find no other path through. We just sort of made our own path, looking for food along the way. Later we discovered some mountain crabs to eat along with flowers and a wild, black mushroom. These sustained us through the jungle until we made it to Thailand. I was pregnant most of the journey. But before we finished, I took a bad fall that killed the baby. We were devastated. But all we could do was cry and keep moving.

We lived in Thailand for three months in a refugee camp. I was having lots of fainting spells, so I spent quite a bit of time in health clinics and hospitals. I was still carrying the dead baby inside. Finally, I fell unconscious. The health workers didn't know how to help me. So they just pulled a sheet over my head as if I had died. But a Catholic priest who was passing through pulled the sheet off my head and told them not to give up on me. I recovered.

A nurse named Carol took compassion on us and helped us find a sponsor in the United States. We made it to Chicago in 1976. Both of our children were born there. By day my husband worked in a bank. At night he worked in a factory.

Three of my siblings died at the hands of the Khmer Rouge. The rest of us all made it to the States.

One day some Mormon missionaries knocked on our door. I liked their message and decided to be baptized with my children. But my husband didn't want to hear about the Church. We went for a while by ourselves. But my husband made things difficult for us. He was abusive. Finally, things got so bad that we got divorced.

I moved my children to Long Beach, California. Here I became a US citizen. We found the Cambodian branch of the Church and could attend without any conflicts. The Church has given my children hope that they can make something of their time on earth. I've had an unusual life with more than my share of problems, but I know the Church is true. The Lord has preserved and prospered my life in so many ways. I will ever be grateful for his loving care.

LYNA THON MOSSHOLDER

My name is Lyna Thon Mossholder. I was born in Kahdown in a refugee camp in 1983. My mom was Thai, and my father was Cambodian. They met while trying to sneak into the camp. He thought she was attractive and very independent and resourceful. It was kind of an unusual match because Thailand and Cambodia are traditionally enemy nations. But they overcame that. They had to teach each other their language so they could communicate. Once they got inside the camp, they still weren't official residents there, so they had to hide. They slept under the hut of some friends they had made that were there officially. Their friends would sneak them food when they could, but the rations were pretty slim as it was. After a lot of finagling, they finally got officially recognized in the camp and move into their own hut. They got married there in the camp. They loved each other and treated each other well. They were good to us as well. They had four children in Thailand and two more after we came to America.

As children growing up in the refugee camp, life was pretty basic. We had a simple school to attend. But mostly we just played. When it rained, we all ran around naked in the mud. And we would swim naked in the dirty, brown river. We had so much fun and nobody cared. We played cards a lot when we could find someone that had some, and we learned to entertain ourselves with whatever we had around.

We didn't have much to eat, and we had no medicines. We bathed in the dirty river. We had to carry water from a public well every day. One time, when I was about four years old, I had severe diarrhea and stomach cramps. They had strange home remedies. They cut my fingers and made me bleed—like the old fashioned bloodletting you see in Jane Austen movies. They poured this awful white liquid on my palms. But the worst were the cigar burns! They used a lit cigar to burn my stomach. To this day, I have six ugly scars where they burned me. It was all part of some horrible folk remedy. But all the kids had to endure it. My brother has the same scars on his stomach from when he got sick.

Life in the camp was hard in many ways. The kids would all scour the fields looking for leftover rice to take home. We'd also catch grasshoppers and eat them. They were such a treat! They tasted crunchy and delicious compared to the plain rice we normally had. Sometimes we caught snakes or rats and cooked them up too. They tasted like chicken. Rats became our family favorite—almost like our specialty. The camp officials would give you extra food if you donated blood. So my dad started donating. Eventually he donated so much that he started having fainting spells. He contracted hepatitis from the needles.

We lived in a straw hut. It had no doors, just curtains. It was dangerous because of the cramped living conditions, and anyone could simply walk into our hut at any time. I remember homes being burned and people dying in the camp. But we survived.

I got picked on a lot in the camp. Other kids gave me mean nicknames all the time. They called me "Ugly Girl" along with a lot of other names taken from nasty, rotten food. They called me "Kape," which means deformed, crippled body. They thought I looked funny with my big head and big stomach. Then one day, my friend and I shook a banana tree trying to get the fruit to fall. Instead we spooked a hive of bees. They came after us in a rage. For some reason, they stung me but not my friend. They swarmed all over my head and stung me over and over. My mother was furious with me. She decided for some reason she needed to shave my head bald. So she did, but she left my bangs. Can you imagine how funny I looked? Everyone thought I was a weirdo then. No one would play with me. Even an old lady who used to watch me sometimes refused to let me come over.

Fortunately, there was one beautiful young lady in her early twenties who recognized my situation and had compassion on me. She was a worker in the refugee camp and took me everywhere. She treated me like a princess. Since everyone liked her, I started getting treated better. When I grew up, I remembered how much that meant to me and have always tried to have compassion on those who are rejected by others.

My dad was a mechanic. He worked mostly on motorcycles because that's what everybody drove. He fixed up two motorcycles for the family. My brother, Sinat, would ride behind my dad, and I would ride behind my mother.

We didn't have many bathrooms in the refugee camp. Mostly we dug and buried. Rich people had them, and there were a few public ones, but you had to walk a long way. One time I used a bathroom by a neighbor's garden. The woman there got very angry and whipped me with a whip made from lemon grass. She beat me so bad that I ended up with scars. After my mother finished cleaning me up, she went and argued with the neighbor. I tried at first to cover up who did it to me because I wasn't the type to tell on folks. But my mother wouldn't let it go until I told.

One night gunshots rang through the camp. I was just a small kid and was terrified. Everyone ran out and left me in the hut crying. No one came back for almost an hour. I had no idea what was going on. My parents got all the other kids out to safety but somehow left me behind. I think they thought my uncle had me, but he didn't. Finally they realized I was missing and sent a man to rescue me. He took me to where everyone else was hiding in the hills outside of camp. We spent the rest of the night there. It was a group of Khmer Rouge robbers that had come to pillage us. They would go through an entire village stealing everything and raping women.

When I was six years old, my parents finally got word that our request for sponsorship was approved. We had to spend six months first in the Philippines, but conditions were better there. We actually had running water and an indoor stove. But finally we made it to Texas, where a YMCA had decided to sponsor us. Coming to the United States was the most exciting thing we ever did. The year was 1989.

Once we made it to the land of the free, my mother told my father that she was divorcing him and taking the kids. He drank and smoke a lot and did not treat her very well. Now she felt like she was going to take advantage of our new freedom and escape from all the tyranny of her past—including him! But before she moved us out, one day there was a knock at the door. It was a pair of Mormon missionaries who said they wanted to teach us about God's plan for families. It was just what we needed to save our family. We listened eagerly and joined the Church. My dad changed his ways and learned how to treat my mom better.

My mom had family in Merced, California, so we eventually moved there to be closer to relatives. The missionaries contacted us, and we started attending church again. But there were more job opportunities for Cambodians in Long Beach, so we soon moved there. Again the missionaries tracked us down and took us to our new branch. It was as if once the Lord had us, he wasn't going to let us go. I grew up in the Park Branch in Long Beach, was baptized when I was eight, and went to Young Women, early-morning seminary, and eventually the young single adult program.

It took a lot to keep our family going. My dad ran an auto repair shop, and my mom ran a Laundromat. They had a lot of financial stresses, which carried over to the family. There was a time when their relationship had grown very strained and there was talk of divorce again. My mom told me that she was going to take the kids and leave. I just fell apart. I left the house sobbing and got into the car and drove, looking for relief. I ended up at the chapel on Xemino Avenue and went inside. There was a picture of the Savior I liked in the foyer, so I stood by it and prayed. I pleaded with the Lord with all my teenage heart to somehow help me keep my family together. I had been clinging to them for my life because I felt as though that was all I had.

I can't remember how long I was there, but eventually something happened.

All of a sudden, I was filled with the Savior's love. I knew he knew who I was and what I was going through and was assured that he would help me through it. I felt like he just wanted me to trust him and things would work out somehow for the best. Whether my parents stayed together or not, I knew now that the Lord would see me through it and I didn't have to worry anymore. My testimony grew tremendously. I realized then that I had more than my family to keep my life together. I had a relationship with a loving Heavenly Father who would sustain me through all the struggles of my life.

Eventually my parents reconciled and put things back together. I was grateful for that, but now I wasn't dependent on them for my survival.

My patriarchal blessing helped me decide to serve a full-time mission. I served on Temple Square in Salt Lake City and loved meeting people from so many different places. For three months, I had the chance to serve in Alaska. I had the privilege of teaching and baptizing the first native Eskimo in that mission in many, many years. The branch president's wife said there was another person I should meet. It was her neighbor—a young man named Chris. But he wasn't a member and wasn't interested in taking the lessons then, so we moved on.

After my mission, Chris surprised me by calling me in Long Beach and telling me he wanted to take the lessons. He did, and a year after I finished my mission, we were sealed in the Newport Beach California Temple in 2006. We tried to find jobs in Long Beach, but we just couldn't make it work. So we moved back to live in Alaska, where Chris already had connections and a good job where they were willing to hire him again. But the Church is true here too. Life hasn't been easy for us, but the Lord has protected us and promised us we can be together forever. One day we'll see that all the suffering in life was worth it.

Sometimes people ask me if I'm still angry over what I had to suffer as a child. But I'm really not. The Khmer Rouge and the guards who mistreated us were just blindly following their leaders. It wasn't personal. Besides, if we didn't suffer so much, we wouldn't have been driven to come to the States. And it's here that we found the gospel that changed and healed our lives. So I really can't wish that any of it were different.

Studying the Book of Mormon has helped me a lot to put together the pieces of my life. It tells the story of Lehi and his family, who had to leave their city to escape destruction—just like we had to leave Cambodia. His family went in search of the promised land and found the Lord, who guided their path. We have paved a similar trail in search of our promised land. Alaska may be a bit colder than Lehi's land of inheritance, but we have found the Lord on our journey as well.

Lyna Thon Mossholder and her new baby, Bryant

HOEUTH LANH

My name is Hoeuth Lanh. I was born in Battambang Province in 1944. I was the second oldest of seven children. When I was a child, my dad would take me into the jungle with him to go fishing. We didn't get the chance to go to school because we had to tend the farm and look after the fruit trees. We had about twelve acres of orchards, where we planted pineapples and oranges. We also had about twenty acres of farmland, where we grew rice and sometimes red corn. I also had the job to herd the cows—we had about forty at the time—and look after the pigs. So between harvesting the fruit and feeding the animals, there was always a lot to keep us busy.

I had a lot of pets as a child. I had twelve crocodiles for a while. I fed them fish, frogs, and crabs. I also had an iguana and two birds of prey, something like eagles. Another time I had a pet tiger cub. It was smart and very friendly. It slept in the house with us. It would go with me to the fields when I worked with my dad. It was very docile and never caused us any problems, but the other villagers were always nervous about him. One day, when my father went off to the jungle, the tiger escaped from his cage and followed him. One of the villagers caught it and ate it. They were always afraid it would attack someone. I cried for two weeks.

The family orchard and farm were two days' walking distance from each other, so depending on the season, I would move from one to the other. During monsoon season I would move to the orchard because the farmland would be flooded. The orchard was considered high land because it didn't flood during monsoons. I would often have to move the cows from one place to the other, depending on the season.

My father was a great man. He was very religious. We were all Buddhists, but one time Christian missionaries came through our little village and gave my father a Bible. He read to me from it every night. We were still Buddhist, but our belief in the Christian God began to grow. One summer, there was a great drought. The animals in the meadows started to die off, and we could smell their stench in our huts. There was no rain for months, and the crops were dying off as well. My father had great faith that God could help us. With other villagers watching, he went out in the middle of one of the fields of dead and dying crops, knelt down, and began pleading with God. It was a scorching hot afternoon without a cloud in the sky. When my father finished his sincere pleading, he stood up and looked at the sky expectantly. We all watched clouds start to form in the sky. Like a gift from heaven, they opened up and started pouring out rain upon the parched land. The people wept in gratitude and joy. Everyone knew that it was the humble faith of my father that worked this saving miracle. They all thanked him for what he had done. I learned from my father that God is aware of his children. He will care for us if we only learn to ask sincerely.

One year our village was hit by a severe illness. We all got high fevers and chills, but eventually we recovered. My dad started to feel better and decided to go back to tend his orchard. Tragically, he had a relapse and passed away. Apparently none of the workers there knew how to help him. I always felt bad that I hadn't been there to nurse him back to health. He was only fifty-seven years old. After they cremated him, we moved back to Battambang a couple of hours away. We took all our cows with us. Along the way, some of the men who were helping us transport the cows decided to steal them. But at the last minute, one of the men had a strong feeling that they shouldn't, and he convinced the others to back off as well. I guess the Lord was helping us all along.

When I was twenty-one, a man came to our home and asked my mother for my hand in marriage. I didn't want to marry him. He was stubborn and had a temper. My mother said to just marry him so I'd have someone to take care of me. So I did. After we got married, my mother and all my siblings moved in with us. In 1970, my husband was required to join the army and was taken from us. We didn't see him again until 1973.

I was twenty-seven with two children when the Khmer Rouge came to power. They took all our land, all our animals, and all our possessions. They kicked us out of our house, and all we could keep was what we could carry as we fled. We went through the jungle, cutting a path with machetes. But the communists had guards pointing their guns at us as we went. All we had to eat was a small bowl of rice a day. There were four people for every one cup of rice. Then you just looked for whatever else you could find. We boiled water chestnuts. We'd catch red army ants and eat those too. When we were lucky, we caught frogs and crabs.

The Khmer Rouge forced us all to move into small villages and to go out and work in the fields. We had to work ten hours a day or more. I had a baby and two small boys, but they made me leave my boys behind to watch themselves while I worked in the field alongside my husband. I would take my baby with me to the fields and carry her on my back. Sometimes I would just dig a hole in the dirt with a little barrier around it to keep the army ants out and then lay the baby down in it all day. What else could I do? If you didn't work because you had a baby, they would kill either you or the baby. We saw hundreds of adults and children die off or be killed. I taught my children to be creative and resourceful in order to survive. If you have the will and determination, you can accomplish almost anything.

In their short time in power, the Khmer Rouge killed off millions of Cambodians. Then the Vietnamese came in and started to take over. With all the fighting and killing going on in the land, most of the food and resources we were finding in the jungle started to disappear. Conditions grew worse and worse. My husband and I decided that we should try to escape to Thailand. We tried to convince some of our family members to go with us, but they wanted to stay.

We agreed that my husband would go ahead and check out the

way. Shortly after, I started out with our children. We walked for a few days and then met up with my husband in the little town of Swai. We continued on together to the town of Snuug. It was raining day and night. One night we were so thirsty when we stumbled on a water hole and drank heartily. In the morning we found several corpses lying there in the water. But we survived. At times we had to trade extra clothing for bowls of rice. We did whatever it took to make it. I carried my baby strapped to my chest and two pails over my shoulders with our few possessions—a pot and some knives. My two little boys just walked along my side.

At one point, I slipped and fell into the river. It took a while for others to help me out, and I was panicked that my baby had drowned. But as they dragged us out, there was my little girl smiling up at me. My heart was overjoyed with gratitude, and I knew that someone was looking out for us. To protect my children from the army ants as they slept, I surrounded them with fire ashes through the night. Otherwise, they would have been eaten alive. All the rain made a lot of mud and slowed us down. But it was only rainwater that kept us from dying of thirst along our twenty-day march. Sometimes what seems like a trial is actually a blessing in disguise.

We had many wild adventures along the way. At one point, we ran into a wealthy doctor who had plenty of food and provisions. Since we were out of food, he offered to trade. He said that he would take my baby for me and raise it as his own. He had no children and always wanted one. I thought my baby would have a better chance of surviving with the doctor than with me. So with much heartache I gave her to him. We were all set to leave without my baby, when at the last moment I reconsidered my decision. I just could not leave my baby with someone else. I knew it would haunt me the rest of my life. I took my baby back. How glad I am now that I made the right decision. Our lives would never have been the same without my daughter.

We pressed onward and eventually reached a little town called Jarome, very close to the Thai border. We were there for a few weeks when my youngest boy wandered off and got lost. I strapped my daughter on my back and went out searching for him. I finally found him in the company of some people. They said they would be happy to keep him and raise him for me. That kind of thing was fairly common with everybody struggling to survive. But I turned them down and took back my son. When he almost died of a bad fever, we traded what gold we had to buy medicines to keep him alive. Our entire mission became to ensure our family survived.

We finally made it to Thailand. We were there in refugee camps for four years. Life seemed so good there compared to what we went through with the Khmer Rouge. We had our own little hut to live in, and the food rations were better. I grew bean sprouts on the side and sold them in the marketplace. We had a school, where they taught us both Cambodian and English as well as math. My children got to attend school finally, and I was so grateful for that.

In 1982, I was pregnant with our third son when we received the news that we had been accepted to go to the United States. The Catholic church agreed to fund our travel costs. But because I was pregnant, they delayed our trip. We had to stay in the Philippines for five months. There we got to continue our education, and my husband and I both found jobs. I worked as a housekeeper, and he worked as a gardener. My oldest son watched the other children while we saved up for our journey to the United States. How we loved the Filipino people for their kindness to us!

Finally our magic day had come. We arrived in Coronton, Texas, in 1984 and settled there for a couple of years. My husband worked as a custodian, and I worked assembling airplane parts. I was reunited with my brother who was living there in Coronton with his wife. They took turns with some other kind neighbors watching our children so we could both work and save up enough money to make something for our struggling family. It was painful for me to leave our children behind as I went to work each day, but we were trying hard to get our family ahead. One day our five-year-old just wept as I went off to work again. I vowed that somehow we would find a way that I could be with them. We struggled with the language, the culture, and the new way of life. But we were grateful to be out of what we left behind in Cambodia.

Eventually we heard that a lot of Cambodians had settled in Long Beach, California. We got excited about being with our own people and decided to save up to make the trek out west. The bus trip actually helped us adapt a bit more to the American way of life. Along the way, we learned to love hamburgers. We were forced to interact with Americans and learned to come out of our protective shell a bit. We realized that to survive, we would have to learn English. And our children started learning English on that bus ride as well.

In Long Beach, there were many familiar faces and lots of help from the other Cambodians there. We banded together to support each other and to create a community. We worked hard to fit in with American society, but it helped to have a familiar support system.

We discovered that my husband's nephew was living close by. He was an interpreter for the LDS Church. He was such a good example of service and kindness. He introduced us to his new faith, and we were impressed. We took the missionary lessons, felt the Spirit, and decided to get baptized. The missionaries and all the members were so kind to us that it was easy to accept their message. They practiced what they preached. Our oldest two children were baptized with us, but our other two were too young. Since that time, the Church has been a big part of my life. I love reading the Book of Mormon and always feel the Spirit when I read. I know it's true. We saved up for years and finally paid off the Catholic church for their help getting us here to the United States. We will always be grateful for their kindness. But it has been Mormonism that has taught us how to be happy and how to be true Christians.

Friendship with members of the Church has been important to me since I first joined. You need to feel connected to people you share things in common with. One sister, Joann Ludloff, really looked after our family. She was always trying to serve us any way she could. My husband had stomach surgery, so Joann would stop by all the time and bring him fresh papaya because it was good for his stomach. Beverly Garlick was my Relief Society president, and she taught me so much about service. I had a friend in our Cambodian ward for years and years. She too had survived the Khmer Rouge, and we understood each other so well. We served together and relied on each other's strength to help through hard times. And then a few years ago, she passed away. I haven't really found another friend like that. But I know the Church is true, so I continue to attend. I try to share my testimony with others and serve them the best I can.

The Cambodian Park Ward has been so good to us all these years. One time they decided to hold a drivers' training course for everyone in the ward who couldn't drive. They invited us all to the ward parking lot so we could take turns behind the wheel. There was a mixture of older adults and young adults. First there was a presentation on basic rules and mechanics of driving. Then they asked for a volunteer to go first while the rest of us stood around in groups watching, chatting, and waiting for our turn. My daughter, Thyda, was standing next to a car talking with her friends while I was about twenty feet away, talking with mine. All of a sudden, I was impressed to tell Thyda to come stand with me. I called her over, but she declined my invitation and said she was fine with her friends. Not thinking much of it, I let it go. But after a short moment I had another impression—this time much stronger—to tell Thyda to come join me. I yelled at her to come to my side immediately. As soon as she started moving away from the parked car, the person who was learning to drive lost control and hit the exact spot on the parked car where my daughter was standing. Both cars were banged up pretty badly. If Thyda had not moved out of the way, she would have been right in the middle of the wreck and might not have survived. I know that prompting was a warning from the Holy Ghost. I am so thankful for the miraculous gifts the Lord pours out to bless our lives. I know he lives and is aware of our needs and continues to watch out for our welfare.

Some of our family has struggled with their faith in the gospel. Thyda and I have clung to each other and to our faith in the Lord to overcome opposition from our family and others. I encouraged Thyda, and she eventually decided to serve a full-time mission. She had to overcome an incredible amount of opposition, but she courageously persisted. She was called to serve in New Jersey and thrived on that experience. We were both blessed so much for her service. After she returned, she went to BYU in Provo. There she had the privilege to teach English as a second language and to work with missionaries from all over the world. She got to teach Cambodian sisters called to serve in the States. My daughter has become a powerful teacher of the restored gospel.

In her last semester at BYU, Thyda met and dated a wonderful young man. They were sealed in the San Diego Temple in 2006. They now have two beautiful children and are raising them strong in the gospel. These little ones will never really know the hell on earth we escaped to find the light, but they will hopefully enjoy the warmth of its rays all their lives.

We have lived in the United States now for twenty-six years. We love America and everything it stands for. We still love our Cambodian culture, but we don't miss the death and destruction we left behind. We will be forever grateful for the freedom and peace we have discovered in this great land. And we will be forever grateful for the direction and reassurance that the true gospel of Christ has given us in our lives. God lives and is watching over us.

Hoeuth and her husband, Bo, with their children (l to r): Pech, Kong, Thyda, Toukna

HOW HELL HAPPENS

Good people cannot read accounts such as the ones in this book without asking the question, "How could anyone ever do something like this to another human being?" If the motive were obvious greed and jealousy, like Cain slaying Abel, we might understand—though still condemn—the atrocities. But to ridicule, starve, torture, and murder innocent men, women, and children with no apparent motive hinders our ability to make sense of the universe. How could masses of people inflict these inhumane crimes on others? All that is good and decent within us shouts out for some kind of explanation.

I am not a historian. But I believe the answer lies in history—both recent and ancient. So I will take up the burden of trying to explain what I think happened by peeking a bit into the past.

I may have oversimplified and missed relevant points, but I hope that by offering at least a partial explanation, I will raise a warning for us all to protect the future of our children.

Cambodia has a long and complicated history. The ninth to the fifteenth centuries AD was the Golden Age of Cambodia. It was the center of the Khmer Empire. Angkor Wat was the empire's main religious temple and remains the country's biggest tourist attraction today. The Khmers reached great heights of cultural attainment. Art and architecture flourished. Although Cambodia was overwhelmingly Buddhist (Mahayana Buddhist until Theravada Buddhism took over the country in the thirteenth century), religious tolerance was the norm, and the Khmers were a basically peaceful people.

The years 1431–1863 were the Dark Ages of Cambodia. The country was dominated by Siam to the West and Vietnam to the East. From 1863–1953, Cambodia accepted protection from France to fend off its invading neighbors and reluctantly became part of French Indochina. When a people feels oppressed, they are often willing to accept help from anyone who offers relief—even when that relief brings a disguised captivity of its own.

During World War II, from 1941–1945, the Japanese briefly occupied Cambodia. They installed Norodom Sihanouk as a puppet king. After the war, the French retook control of the country but allowed Sihanouk to continue as king. Many young Cambodian intellectuals went to Europe to study and became exposed to communism. They returned home, formed a secret student communist movement, and began to stir up peasants with their anti-imperialist, anti-establishment rhetoric. They called themselves the Khmer Rouge. Pol Pot was one of these idealistic leaders.

In 1953, France finally granted Cambodia its independence, and King Sihanouk took the credit. Once Cambodia had its freedom from the French, Pol Pot and the communists lost a lot of their influence. Through the 1950s and 1960s, Norodom Sihanouk ruled the country. King Sihanouk was eccentric and profligate in his lifestyle, but he traveled the country to mingle with the people and became quite popular. While most historians say he was egocentric and opportunistic, courting the favor of anyone who promised to secure his power, the people liked his charm and rhetoric. He married a beauty queen, and she became popular as well. The communists continued an underground resistance movement to Sihanouk's regime. There was political jockeying from other sides as well, and in 1960, Sihanouk was demoted to prince. But he retained his supreme control of the Cambodian government.

But then came the Vietnam War, and with it, the influence of the United States. Sihanouk allowed North Vietnam to build bases in eastern Cambodia to aid the Chinese in sending support to their cause against South Vietnam. The gesture was more an attempt to court Chinese favor than any genuine support for their Vietnamese rivals, but it resulted in turning the United States against Cambodia.

From 1969 to 1973, the United States conducted bombing raids in Cambodia, targeting Viet Cong communist bases along the border between Cambodia and Vietnam. As the Viet Cong spread to other towns in Cambodia for refuge, the US bombing campaign spread as well. The United States played right into the communists' hands by bombing the countryside. It wasn't difficult for the Khmer Rouge to convince folks who the enemy was as long as the United States was dropping bombs on their villages and killing their friends and families. US efforts to explain itself by saying, "It's not you we're after—it's the North Vietnamese hiding among you that we want" fell on deaf ears.

In 1970, Prince Sihanouk was visiting Beijing, courting Chinese support, when the top military commander in Cambodia, General Lon Nol, seized power in a military coup. With US support, he declared a new Khmer Republic. When Prince Sihanouk returned, a civil war broke out between the military regime supported by the United States and the Khmer Rouge communists, who were supported by the Viet Cong of North Vietnam. Prince Sihanouk, seeking to regain power, decided to join the communists and came out in open support of them. Most of those recruited to fight for the Khmer Rouge thought they were fighting to restore Prince Sihanouk to power. But Pol Pot, the leader of the Khmer Rouge, and his elite circle of cohorts had different plans.

With their peasant army, the Khmer Rouge took control of the capital city of Cambodia, Phnom Penh, in April 1975. They reinstated Prince Sihanouk as sort of a puppet king held in detention, but Pol Pot took control of the country as Prime Minister. He quickly began to drive out all foreign influence and to set up a self-sufficient, rural society run by his elite circle of friends on behalf of the peasants. When Sihanouk finally saw the folly of what the Khmer Rouge had set out to accomplish, he resigned and went into exile in China.

From the beginning, the communists recruited poor farmers for support. They promised to eliminate class distinctions and to share the country's wealth with everyone. But in the end, communist nations never rise much above the poverty level for their people. The equality they produce is poverty for everyone—not prosperity. If people are free to control their own destiny, they rise to the level of their own abilities and efforts. But that inevitably leaves some behind. Communism appeals to those left behind. It promises, "We'll take care of you, and you won't have to work harder. If you just support us as your leaders, you can have what all these other folks have but without the effort."

The communist leaders became a law unto themselves. They convinced everyone that they represented the best interests of the people,

so anyone who opposed them was the enemy. Traditional morality as taught by religion and in the schools was just an example of capitalist prejudices imposed over the working class poor to keep them in line. The only way to equalize the former differences was to purge the country of all semblances of the old morality. Once the old way was labeled as "evil," any methods used to rid the country of it seemed to be justified. The guardians of the old way were killed as enemies of the new state. This was just a practical application of the communist slogan: "Anything which furthers the cause of communism is moral."

Once the Khmer Rouge took power in the capital city of Phnom Penh, they quickly set about deconstructing the old societal structures in order to build their envisioned utopia. They named their new state Kampuchea. They believed the educated city dwellers had all been corrupted by Western capitalist ideology. They distrusted anyone who might be inclined to think for himself. That included all professionals, so hospitals, schools, and universities were all shut down. They wanted to wipe out any remnants of capitalism or imperialism, so all factories and banks were closed. All religion was abolished. Thousands of Buddhist monks were slaughtered. Television was eliminated. All forms of music and radios were banned. Money was abolished. All foreign influence was outlawed. Embassies were closed. Children were taken from their parents at age eight to be indoctrinated in communist ideology. They were taught to be loyal to the state instead of the old ways of culture, religion, and family. The promise of freedom from hard work was quickly forgotten. People were required to work in the fields from 4:00 a.m. to 10:00 p.m. and given only one day in ten to rest. Picking fruit out in the wild (even though you were starving) was labeled private enterprise and punishable by execution.

While the Viet Cong communists in North Vietnam shared with their Khmer Rouge communists next door a hatred for America, they didn't trust each other. Old rivalries resurfaced, and Pol Pot repeatedly conducted raids over the border. North Vietnam retaliated. In 1979, they invaded Phnom Penh, drove Pol Pot and the Khmer Rouge into the jungles on the western border with Thailand, and set up a puppet government they called the People's Republic of Kampuchea. Civil war continued between forces loyal to this government and the Khmer Rouge until the United Nations finally sponsored elections in 1993.

From the very beginning, the Khmer Rouge promised the people of

Cambodia freedom—freedom from the French, from the Vietnamese, from the United States, and from any other capitalists, imperialists, or foreigners. They were able to convince the rural farmers that all their troubles were caused by the imperialist capitalists symbolized by the United States. The communists would liberate their country from foreign control and give the power back to the people.

Most of the early Khmer Rouge recruits were children and teenagers. Many were eager to give up working long, unfruitful hours on the farm for the excitement of the military. At those impressionable ages, they were more easily brainwashed into doing what their leaders wanted in the name of the common good. "You may not understand why you're doing what we're making you do, but just trust us that it will be for the greater good." The lyrics of a song by a Russian, Bulat Okudzhava, capture some of what these young Khmer Rouge must have felt:

The Song of a Happy Soldier
I'll take a bag, a helmet and a ration,
A jacket of protective coloration,
I'll tramp about the streets, a barracks lodger,
It's easy to become a real soldier.

I will forget my daily cares and pledges,
I do not have to think of jobs and wages.
I'm playing with my gun, a barracks lodger,
It's easy to become a real soldier.

If something should go wrong, I do not care.
It's, so to say, my Motherland's affair.
It's great to be a simple barracks lodger,
An innocent and inoffensive soldier.

There seems to be in human nature a desire to abdicate responsibility for making difficult choices to an authority figure. At the same time, we are easily tempted by anyone who promises to give us power and influence in the world.

But it's not just youth that are susceptible to the tyranny of misplaced authority figures and the enticement of unearned influence. In the early 1960s, a psychologist, Stanley Milgram, ran a series of experiments at Yale University to show how submission to authority figures can overcome our sense of morality. Milgram set up a scenario where the participants had to push a button they thought was administering a shock to a person in another room to help them learn faster. He showed that 65 percent of participants would administer a fatal shock to a supposed victim if told to do so by a researcher, even though they could hear supposed cries for mercy by the supposed victims (played by convincing actors). In a variation on the experiment, when participants first watched others supposedly administering shock to victims, the participants assumed that it must be acceptable and would go further themselves. Ninety percent administered the deadly shock. All of the participants were normal, mainstream American adults. The Milgram shock experiments were duplicated with similar results in countries across the world—even thirty-five years later. Apparently, most of us run the risk of suppressing what our moral conscience tells us is wrong when told to do so by an authority figure.

But how does all this history and psychology explain how someone could kill an innocent child? Wouldn't it take a monster to allow one's sense of morality to be turned off to that extreme? While I was writing this essay and contemplating how this mass destruction could have happened, I saw a baby spider on the wall. It was innocent, doing no harm to anyone. I thought to myself, "I should leave it alone." But then I said, "No, he will grow quickly and multiply, and soon our house will be overrun by such spiders." I smashed it against the wall with a piece of paper. As I did, I said silently to the spider, "Sorry, my friend, but I have to do this." And I didn't have anyone urging me on in my task of destruction.

I wonder if communist executioners didn't go through dilemmas similar to this as they were instructed to kill innocent babies. "These are children of the enemy who will grow to become part of the enemy. Better to eliminate them now. Better even for their sakes to keep them from being wrongly indoctrinated by the enemy and forever perverted in their training. It is all for the protection of the State." All that has to happen is for the enforcers to be convinced that their actions are for the greater good. Then with righteous zeal, they will carry out any demonic plans with minimal complaints, all the while masking the pangs of conscience with rhetoric and ideology. Once they start down this path, fear of being executed themselves for disobedience can keep them performing their "duty."

In the War in Heaven, Satan was able to convince a third of

Heavenly Father's children that he had the better plan. He offered limitless freedom with no responsibility. We can almost hear him saying, "If the Father's plan of full agency is enacted, there will be winners and losers, and everyone will fare according to their own abilities and efforts. But if you go with my plan, I'll take care of you no matter how incompetent you may be, and you will get the same reward as everyone else." Of course, the captivity in such a plan was hidden. The captivity would come in making all a slave to their appetites and thus easily manipulated. But Satan was so convincing that he was able to persuade a third part of the children of the living God to wage a war against their Maker, demanding their rights. This is the communist way, with revolutions to overthrow the existing governments, promising freedom but seeking only power and dominion over the masses. The First Presidency stated in a message in 1942, "Communism and all other similar isms . . . are merely the clumsy counterfeits which Satan always devises of the Gospel plan."[1]

Even as communism's lure in society has mostly subsided due to its concrete failures in Russia and Eastern Europe, these deceptive tactics it used are still part of Satan's counterfeit plan with young people today. "Your parents make you work too hard," he tells them. "They are glutting themselves on your labors. You should be free to do as you please. You shouldn't have to work so hard for nothing. Your parents are just keeping you down. No one should reject you for doing what you want. I'll love you no matter what." But in place of the universal salvation, what he really offers is universal captivity. Once people buy into his promise of freedom to do what they want, they find themselves enslaved by their appetites. The rising generation too often lacks the experience and insight to see the inconsistencies and irrationality of Satan's claims. His real goal is "to blind men, and to lead them captive at his will" (Moses 4:4). The Father's plan maximizes agency, accountability, and self-control. Only then can each individual have the opportunity to become all that they have in them to become. Satan's plan uses half-truths to distract people from the real issues and disguises the captivity and misery he has in store for them.

So how does hell happen? It happens whenever we get lazy and slip into the temptation to allow others to think for us, to expect others to work for us, or to demand that others suffer for us. The only remedy is eternal vigilance, to remain on guard against any idea or event or individual or group that promises salvation while encouraging our baser passions or dulling our sensitivity to others and to God. Salvation comes only through the harmony between Christ's atonement and our own righteous use of agency. There is no other way.

It would be natural to respond to the perpetrators of violence with resentment and a desire for revenge. The atrocities levied out by the communists in Cambodia (as well as the fascists in Germany) deserve to be punished! But what the heroes of these survival and conversion stories have shown us is that the answer never lies in revenge. To give in to our resentment would simply nurture the same impulses that led to the original atrocities—the urge to blame others for our problems. As Gandhi once taught, "An eye for an eye makes the whole world blind." Besides, the Khmer Rouge soldiers, mostly recruited as children, were, in a very real way, victims themselves of their leaders' brainwashing. The only Christian answer to abuse is forgiveness. Forgiveness doesn't preclude the possibility of accountability, and we certainly must hold those responsible accountable. But it is forgiveness that frees us from the hate and oppression of anger and stops the cycle of abuse. It will be the righteousness of the saints that binds Satan in the Millennium (see 1 Ne. 22:26). It won't be force or compulsion that will win the day. It will be the final triumph of love.

Note
1. Conference Report, April 1942, 88–97.

WHAT ASTRONOMERS KNOW

by Shoni Conrad

Once a summer,
comes a night of shooting stars,
inspiring tourists
and astronomers to travel
to the darkest places.

Always,
the gift of darkness
has been light,

has been God.

Who
after all,
will recognize him
more completely
than those who have grown in the dark,
leaning toward imaginings of light,
waiting,
with all their candled hopes burning,
filaments
in the broad night?

ABOUT THE AUTHOR

Penne Conrad (1942–2010) was a real estate agent, real estate appraiser, and businesswoman. But most of all, she was a wife and a mother. She and her husband, Mike, had four children and fourteen grandchildren. Penne had a love of missionary work her whole life. She served as a stake and ward missionary with her husband for fifteen years, working with the Park Branch (later the Park Ward) in Long Beach, California, and also with two different young single adult wards. She had the gift that all great souls have of making everyone who knew her feel as though they were the most important person in the world to her. Penne also knew something of suffering: She successfully fought off cancer three times. She died of liver failure.